# The
# Irrelevant
# English
# Teacher

# The
# Irrelevant
# English
# Teacher

J. Mitchell Morse

TEMPLE UNIVERSITY PRESS

*Philadelphia*

To Frances

TEMPLE UNIVERSITY PRESS, PHILADELPHIA 19122

© 1972 by Temple University
All rights reserved. Published 1972
Printed in the United States of America

Second Printing 1973
International Standard Book Number: 0-87722-016-6

Library of Congress Catalog Card Number: 72-80762

3- 16 -73

# *Contents*

# Preface

To the extent that the establishment depends on the inarticulacy of the governed, good writing is inherently subversive.

That's why many students never learn to write well. The difficulty is less intellectual than psychological.

Black English, the shuffling speech of slavery, serves the purposes of white racism.

Silent-majority white English serves the purposes of black racism.

We are perishing for lack of style.

Style is a matter of intellectual self-respect. To write well, a certain moral courage is essential. A certain insouciance.

Literary judgment is not a matter of feeling but a matter of intellectual perception. This too takes courage. And knowledge.

Good writing is relevant to itself. It need not be relevant to anything else.

Bad writing is not relevant to itself, or to anything else.

The difference between good writing and bad is objectively demonstrable.

The contemplation of a well-made sentence is the second greatest pleasure in life. The greatest, of course, is to write such a sentence oneself. What did you think it was?

There are people who sit down at the dinner table and start thinking about cholesterol. When they open a novel they start thinking about its political relevance. They shouldn't teach English. Full professors should teach freshman English.

These are the themes that will appear in the succeeding pages. They emerged gradually through my experiences as a teacher, and were developed in a series of articles and speeches, which now constitute this book.

At the time I wrote chapter 1 the word "Negro" was still used by people of decent instincts; the expression "the blacks," on the other hand, was used by British colonialists and American white trash: in Margaret Bourke-White's and Erskine Caldwell's *You Have Seen Their Faces* (1937), a chain-gang guard is quoted as saying, "Beat a dog and he'll obey you. They say it's the same with the blacks." By the time I wrote chapter 7 linguistic fashion had reversed these usages, and I conformed to the reversal without a qualm. The verbal inconsistency reflects an emotional consistency.

The death of Nasser since I wrote chapter 2 doesn't affect the argument. Simply substitute the name Gromyko.

Chapter 1 appeared as an article in *College English,* an organ of the National Council of Teachers of English. It resulted in an invitation to speak at the University of Wisconsin, Milwaukee, as one of a weekly series of speakers on contemporary trends. The text of that speech—which also appeared in *College English*—is chapter 2. Since the previous speaker had been John Hendrick Clarke, editor of *William Styron's Nat Turner: Ten Black Writers Respond,* I was asked to illustrate my thesis by referring to Styron's *The Confessions of Nat Turner.* I could hardly have chosen a better illustration; I am grateful to the organizers of the series, Professors Neal Riemer (political science) and Richard Peltz (philosophy) for suggesting it.

Chapters 3 and 4 appeared in *The CEA Critic,* an organ of the College English Association; chapter 5 was rejected by some half-dozen magazines, for reasons that will be apparent to all who read it; chapter 6 was read by invitation at the 1969 meeting of the National Council of Teachers of English, and later appeared in

*College English;* chapter 7 will appear in a future issue of *College English;* a shorter version of chapter 8 was read at the 1970 meeting of the College English Association; chapter 9 was commissioned by, and appeared in, *College English;* chapter 10 appeared in *The English Record,* organ of the New York State Council of Teachers of English; a shorter version of chapter 11 appeared in *Twelve and a Tilly,* edited by Jack P. Dalton and Clive Hart (Faber and Faber and The Viking Press, 1966). To the editors and publishers of these publications I am grateful for permission to reprint.

I owe a special debt of gratitude to Anne-Marie Chancholle-Rajon, who introduced me to Bossuet.

And every page of the book is indebted to my wife, Frances, but for whose intelligence, wit, courage and love there would be no book.

*The*
*Irrelevant*
      *English*
*Teacher*

# The Case for Irrelevance

In the classroom, I preach irrelevance. I once knew a professor of chemical engineering, a deeply religious man but a conscientious teacher, who regretted that he could find no way to promote Christian values through his courses. As a secular political liberal I share his sense of frustration; for as a teacher of literature I find that the best thing I can do for political liberalism in class is to ignore it. This is not a paradox.

I am very much concerned with civil rights and the war in Vietnam; I believe that the enemies of reform are the friends of revolution; I believe that those on the right who refuse to permit the correction of intolerable conditions by democratic means are unwitting allies and dupes of those on the left who preach that they cannot be corrected by democratic means; I wish that good novelists, playwrights and poets would address themselves to these problems; but alas, with a few brilliant exceptions such as Günter Grass, Peter Weiss and Heinrich Böll, they leave that job to writers who have more heart than art; and as an English teacher I cannot with any conscience invite my students to read kitsch as literature or literature as sociology. I will not tell them that *MacBird* is a great play. I will not tell them that *Another Country* is a great novel, or even a good one. I will not suggest that they read *Paradise Lost* as a political document. And I will not tell them that reading "Go, Lovely Rose" is a waste of time. Relevance be damned, I say. As a teacher of literature, I think it is vitally important for my students to develop some sensitivity to literary values; as an individual and I hope as a citizen, I fight, in class and out, against the calculated insensitivity of the all-out political mind. I fear that mind. Whatever side it's on, it's against me. It would tell me what to read and what not to read, what to enjoy and what not to enjoy, what to teach and what not to teach. It would have me rate Carl Sandburg above Wallace Stevens, and Arthur Koestler above Samuel Beckett. It is the enemy of nuance; and where nuances are suppressed I can't live.

I know, I know. I would not presume to tell a Negro product of white racism, unemployed and demoralized to the point of being unemployable, that he should be reasonable or have a sense of humor or an appreciation of nuances. He is not in a reasonable situation, much less an amusing one. As for nuances, I myself think it is fatuous to make fine distinctions between George Wallace and William Buckley, Jr. Teach George to say "Cui bono?" and "mutatis mutandis," and he too would be a right-wing intellectual. But to lump me with them, merely because I am white, is to overlook essential differences, to say nothing of nuances; and to tell me that when I take the time to enjoy "Go, Lovely Rose" or "Thirteen Ways of Looking at a Blackbird" I am being immoral is to be an enemy of civilization. That demoralized Negro is an enemy of civilization because he can't afford not to be. He can no more live with nuances than I can live without them; they threaten him as much as lack of them threatens me. In this intellectual separatism there is no future for either of us. If he is driven to destroy what I stand for, he will not thereby liberate himself: for a society that cannot tolerate poems that have nothing to recommend them but beauty will not be led by people with decent instincts. And neither will my values be preserved if that Negro is destroyed or suppressed. A society that suppresses him will suppress me. The rednecked cop licensed to kill him is no friend of my civil, intellectual or academic freedom, or my right to live; nor are the authorities in whose name he shoots. Between George Wallace and William Buckley, Jr., on the one hand,

and Rap Brown and Stokely Carmichael on the other, I see nothing
to choose.

Our society's general unconcern with literary values has had
unfortunate effects on the whole quality of its life, including its
moral quality and ultimately its political quality. For years I have
been distressed by the popularity of that cornball Ayn Rand among
undergraduate students, and by their enthusiasm for her as a thinker.
The process of disabusing them has to begin when they ask their first
question, always the same, "Is Ayn Rand considered a good writer?"
"Yes," I have learned to say. "By millions of people. Is that what
you mean?" Some say, "No, I mean . . ." and stop, stuck. They can't
even conceive the real question. Others, who can't conceive it either,
say, "No. I mean, like, do *you* consider her a good writer?" The real
question, "*Is* she a good writer?" doesn't occur to them. It surprises
them. They don't believe in it. They believe in opinion, not in the
possibility of true judgment; and they believe that the only
difference between one man's opinion and another's is—well, like
there's experts: like an English prof, for example, can tell better
than like a business man. Can tell what better? Like whether the
book is "considered good." I quote.

It is very hard to break this enchanted circle. It is very hard to
induce a course of thinking that makes sense. But there are certain
things we can do, and certain things we must not do. In terms of
politics, *Strange Fruit* is as good as *A Passage to India;* for this
reason, as well as for obvious tactical reasons, we must not argue
about Ayn Rand's politics. All such arguments are beside the point.
We must concentrate on her corny prose. And we must juxtapose it
with examples of good prose. We don't absolutely have to start with
a meditation by John Donne. There are more accessible examples all
around us, including many that are not associated with the scare
word "literature." There are even familiar jokes that will serve our
purpose. Even bad jokes. For some bad jokes are good: that's why
we enjoy them. The tactless question King Arthur asked Queen
Guenevere, "Who was that last knight I seen you with, lady?" is a
good bad joke. We call it low, we loudly profess not to enjoy it, but
we do enjoy it. Good bad jokes, good good jokes, good nursery
rhymes, good novels, and good translations of poetry and literary

prose—as we shall see—are all good for the same reason: they give us literary pleasure. With regard to literature, pleasure and judgment are inseparable: if the work gives us pleasure, we call it good; if it doesn't, or if we wish it didn't (and this is a complication I'll explain away in a few minutes), we call it incompetent or cheap or low or pretentious or meretricious.

Every judgment is an estimate of effectiveness: a good scientific theory is one that works, a good highway surface is one that stands up to the traffic and the changes of weather, a good paint is one that lasts and keeps its appearance, and a good work of art is one that gives us pleasure. This last item seems to be affected by a degree of subjectivity that doesn't affect the others; but it isn't. For with regard to a work of art we must distinguish the pleasure it gives us through its own qualities from the other pleasures it may suggest. Every aesthetic judgment involves such a distinction.

Any representation or suggestion of sexuality, for example, be it a painting, a statue, a piece of music, a dance, a film, or a poem, will give us intimations, however faint, of erotic pleasure; but if it is well made, each will give us in addition an aesthetic pleasure peculiar to itself, which it does not share with the others: graphic pleasure, plastic pleasure, musical pleasure, choreographic pleasure, cinematic pleasure, literary pleasure.

Literary pleasure has to do with words: it is the pleasure that a skillful performance with words affords us, whether or not we consciously observe it. When we do consciously observe it we are likely to enjoy it more, because our consciousness of what is going on doesn't inhibit or replace our unconscious emotional response but supplements it and may even serve to arouse it. I didn't respond emotionally to Marvell's

>           Annihilating all that's made
>           To a green thought in a green shade

until I understood it intellectually—several years after I first read it: only then, having begun to read Plato, did I suddenly see what Marvell was doing, and the joy of a complex and subtle perfection flooded my eyes. All our educationists notwithstanding, intellectual perception does not deaden emotional response; often the emotional response depends absolutely on the intellectual perception. Accordingly, an unintended perception is liable to produce an unintended response. If a lyric offers nothing for our intellect to perceive but the fact that it is making a cliché appeal to our tears, we will respond not with tears but with a smile of amusement or a sigh of boredom or a moment of resentment at the effort to take us in. The possibility that the effort was made unconsciously, with all naive good will, is not likely to increase our respect for the hack who made it. He is afflicted with what Plato called the lie in the soul.

The intensity of our pleasure in a literary performance depends on the degree of skill it manifests and on our ability to perceive skill. These are two different things: each may operate independently of the other, and each may exceed the other. We call jokes "low," for example, when the degree of skill is so slight that we are ashamed to be so easily pleased: the joke is facile, the pleasure is low-grade. In the following illustrative story, our ability to perceive the verbal cleverness is so far in excess of the cleverness itself that we feel ruefully that we have been had:

> Once upon a time there were two little skunks named In and Out. One day In went out and didn't come in, so their mommy said to Out, "Out, go out and bring In in." So out went Out, and after a while, sure enough, he brought in In. Do you know how he found him? In stinked.

In this case, when I say that we have been had I don't mean that we have been abused, as has the person who gives a merely sentimental response to a cliché lyric. I mean that our response, however slight, was more than such a weak performance deserved. Nevertheless, we do respond: we respond with pleasure, not to the ostensible content, but to the arrangement of words. Change the names of the skunks, or change "stinked" to "stunk," and though the plot remains unchanged the story ceases to have any interest. Our interest, our pleasure, however low, is purely literary.

The opposite case, in which the skill of the performance gives us

pleasure even though we may have no ability to perceive skill, is
illustrated by the nursery rhyme

> One misty moisty morning,
> When cloudy was the weather,
> I chanced to meet an old man
> Clothed all in leather.
>
> He began to compliment
> And I began to grin:
> "How do you do?" and
> "How do you do?"
> And "How do you do?" agin.

Like many of the Mother Goose rhymes, this one is pure poetry.
Little children love it long before they learn to read, long before
they know the meaning of the word "compliment," long before they
become clearly conscious of the alliterations, assonances, con-
sonances and repetitions that make it good. They respond with
physiological pleasure to these products of physiological play in the
author—who also, as we know, need not have been clearly conscious
of what was going on inside himself. Or herself. Like the poets
whom Socrates interviewed, he or she may very well have been less
able to account for the quality of the poem than any of us academic
bystanders.

Another kind of literary pleasure comes of solving verbal puzzles
or seeing them solved: that is, of joining the author in a word game.
The familiar palindromes Joyce puts in the mouth of Lenehan in
*Ulysses*—"Madam, I'm Adam" and "Able was I ere I saw Elba"—and
the various games he plays in *Finnegans Wake*—such portmanteaus as
"Puffedly offal" and "that farced epistol to the hibruws," the
imitative form of "bi tso fbrok engl a ssan dspl itch ina," the
colorful image of Jarl von Hoother charging out of his castle "like a
rudd yellan gruebleen orangeman in his violet indigonation," and the
linguistic miming of Mutt and Jute—

> Scuse us, chorley guy! You tollerday donsk? N. You tolkatiff
> scowegian? Nn. You spigotty anglease? Nnn. You phonio saxo? Nnnn.

Clear all so! Tis a Jute. Let us swop hats and excheck a few strong
verbs weak oach eather yapyazzard abast the blooty creeks. . . .[1]

—these and other such puzzles have in each case a formal integrity
that is content enough, and to which we respond with pleasure. But
a trick is after all a source of rather low-grade pleasure: the pleasure
of not having been tricked or of seeing belatedly how the trick
worked. This is true even when the trick is more subtle, as when
Beckett says in *Watt* that the busy Mr. Spiro could cite many
theologians "because he was a man of leisure"—i.e., a scholar, the
word *scholar* being a derivative of the Greek *scholé,* leisure, and our
pleasure in the sentence depending absolutely on our knowledge of
this fact.[2] Sometimes Beckett's tricks are subtler still, as when he
says on page 202 of the Grove Press edition of *Murphy* that Wylie
sought Murphy as a means of marrying Miss Counihan because
(among other attractions) "she had private means," and on page 213
makes Wylie say to the other self-seeking seekers, "Our medians, or
whatever the hell they are, meet in Murphy."[3] But this kind of
thing, though much more sophisticated than the bad joke about
King Arthur and Queen Guenevere, gives us essentially the same
simple kind of pleasure—tainted, moreover, with the emulation that
seems to be an inescapable aspect of puzzle-solving: a non-aesthetic
pleasure.

Pure, non-emulative and intense or high literary pleasure comes of
observing a performance that exercises without baffling our ability
to perceive literary skill, and in which—as in a handsome wrought

---

1. From *Finnegans Wake* by James Joyce. Copyright © 1939 by James
Joyce, © by George Joyce and Lucia Joyce. Reprinted by permission of The
Viking Press, Inc., and of The Society of Authors. This acknowledgment
applies to all other quotations from *Finnegans Wake* throughout this book.

2. In book V, chapter XXX, of *Pantagruel,* Rabelais speaks of Aristotle,
Porphyry, etc., "et . . . cinq cens autres gens aussi de loisir." (See the Garnier
Classics edition of the *Oeuvres Complètes,* II, 399.) The Motteux translation
of book V, which is the one most of us read, renders this passage "five
hundred other such plodding dons, who were full of business, yet had little to
do." It's Rabelaisian, but it isn't Rabelais; it obscures the ambiguity that
Rabelais and Beckett intended.

3. From *Murphy* by Samuel Beckett. First published 1938; first Grove
Press edition 1957. Copyright © 1957 by Grove Press. Reprinted by
permission of Grove Press, Inc. This acknowledgment applies to all quotations
from *Murphy* throughout this book.

iron gate with a design of vine leaves and tendrils—form and content so perfectly express each other that the form seems natural, the content artful, and both inevitable. What Joyce and Beckett afford us is essentially this pleasure, to which all their tricks are only incidental. Joyce's description in *Ulysses* of the priest rising from the water owes its quality to the exact rightness—the literary justice—of every word, not to any trick:

> An elderly man shot up near the spur of rock a blowing red face. He scrambled up by the stones, water glistening on his pate and on its garland of grey hair, water rilling over his chest and paunch and spilling jets out of his black sagging loincloth.[4]

If the word "scrambled," for example, were changed to "clambered" or "climbed" or "crawled" or "struggled" or "pulled himself" or any other near equivalent, the content would be changed, the moving image would be less vivid and would not suggest as it does just what it does. An ordinary writer might have said, "An oldish man emerged from the water near a spur-like rock, red-faced and puffing. He clambered up over the stones, wet from head to foot." A somewhat better writer might have added, "with [*sic,* fatally *sic*] water gleaming on his bald head encircled with grey hair, running down over his pot-bellied body, and pouring copiously out of his sagging, black loincloth." The ostensible content—the intended content, the priest himself—is the same in this passage as in Joyce's; but the actual content—the representation of the priest—is of much poorer quality and gives us a much poorer pleasure. Joyce's representation shows the priest alive; the other makes him—if you'll pardon my saying this of a priest—only a lay figure. Joyce's superiority lies in his more accurate choice of words: "blowing," "glistening," "pate," "rilling," "spilling," "chest and paunch," "from"; in his repetition of "water," and in the greater speed and more appropriate emphasis of "black sagging" without a comma.

---

4. From *Ulysses* by James Joyce. Copyright © 1914, 1918 by Margaret Caroline Anderson and renewed 1942, 1946, by Nora Joseph Joyce. Copyright © 1934 by The Modern Library, Inc. Reprinted by permission of Random House, Inc. This acknowledgment applies to all quotations from *Ulysses* throughout this book.

Beckett's language is equally just, and usually more formal. He is a descendant of the great medieval stylists, who embodied in the rhetorical devices of classic decorum a most unclassic vehemence of feeling; but he goes far beyond them in the strictness of his rules, for to the difficulty of conveying private feeling through the syntactic gestures of public ceremony he adds the difficulty of refusing to use what Joyce called "big words": such words as "love," "grief," "despair," "alas," etc., which the medieval stylists used with a freedom that amounted to abandon and debauchery. Except for purposes of humor, when he often uses rare and even exotic words, Beckett restricts himself to the vocabulary of simple concreteness. The following three paragraphs, from a passage telling us how Watt passed the evenings in his room, constitute a perfect poem, with a beginning, a middle and an end, whose classic balance and pragmatic vocabulary convey a lyric intensity of feeling that hotter and smokier words and a more romantic syntax might perhaps parody but could surely not match:

> At ten the steps came, clearer, clearer, fainter, fainter, on the stairs, on the landing, on the stairs again, and through the open door the light, from darkness slowly brightening, to darkness slowly darkening, the steps of Arthur, the light of poor Arthur, little by little mounting to his rest, at his habitual hour.
>
> At eleven the room darkened, the moon having climbed behind a tree. But the tree being small, and the moon's ascension rapid, this transit was brief, and this obscuration.
>
> As by the steps, the light, growing, dying, Watt knew that it was ten, so he knew, when the room darkened, that it was eleven, or thereabouts.[5]

The purely literary beauty of this passage is clear to anyone who has any acquaintance at all with the classic mode or any intuitive sensitivity to form; but to say that it moves us by its form alone would be false. We are also moved by the loneliness of Watt and

5. From *Watt* by Samuel Beckett, all rights reserved; originally published by The Olympia Press, Paris, 1953; first Grove Press edition, 1959; reprinted by permission of The Grove Press, Inc., and of Calder and Boyars, London. This acknowledgement applies to all quotations from *Watt* throughout this book.

Arthur, which though not mentioned is made unmistakably evident through the imagery, the rhythm and the vocabulary that don't mention it. So that our pleasure in the passage is a complex of three elements: (1) an intellectual appreciation of its form, (2) an emotional appreciation of its unstated content as well as of the physiological play that underlies it, and (3) a secondary intellectual appreciation of the skill with which the content is suggested and our feelings are touched.

The second element, though non-literary insofar as it concerns the content, is not sentimental. It is a real emotion, honestly evoked; for honesty in literature requires indirection. A direct appeal to our sentimentality is liable to be meretricious; if it lacks validity of form, it will inevitably be meretricious. Consider, for example, these verses by Bayard Taylor:

> From the Desert I come to thee
> On a stallion shod with fire;
> And the winds are left behind
> In the speed of my desire.
> Under thy window I stand
> And the midnight hears my cry:
> I love thee! I love but thee!
> With a love that shall not die
> *Till the sun grows cold,*
> *And the stars are old,*
> *And the leaves of the Judgment*
> *Book unfold!*

Why did Taylor capitalize "Desert"? For the same reason that he italicized the last three verses: in order to make the corn grow taller. He was proud of effects he should have been ashamed of. Homer's heroes pursued each other with winged feet, addressed each other with winged words, and shot each other with winged arrows: "The winged arrow smote him in the throat, and his limbs were all unstrung, and he groveled in the dust." The metaphor is not always so clearly visual, but it always makes a legitimate analogy. But what is the meaning of "shod with fire"? I make an effort to see that stallion's feet, and what I see doesn't make sense. How speedy is desire? To outstrip one wind of any speed worth talking about would be quite a feat in itself, but to outstrip them all without riding in all directions takes genius. If the stars are not old by this time, when will they be? And why intimate that such love will die just when eternity is about to begin? Shakespeare, promising his beloved that he/she would live in memory for the duration of the English language, was both more modest and more confident.

Bayard Taylor was a respectable citizen who surely had no intention of making a meretricious appeal; he was not a writer of schlock books; but these verses have the appeal of a torch singer in a Grade F night club or a prostitute under a street lamp luring the farm boys; and now that I'm quoting Carl Sandburg let me say that his poem about Chicago makes the same kind of appeal. Certainly Sandburg's idiom is superior to Taylor's, but it too is a thing of hot and smoky words—"Stormy, husky, brawling"—and nonsensical abstractions—"Flinging magnetic curses amid the toil of piling job on job"—plus Chamber-of-Commerce bombast: "Freight Handler to the Nation." What makes this last phrase ridiculous is the disparity of form and content. The British tradesmen's formula, "By appointment to H.M. the Queen," retains an earlier use of "to" that expressed a relationship not only private but personal, as when Congreve designated Mrs. Fainall as "Daughter to Lady Wishfort, and Wife to Fainall, formerly Friend to Mirabell." The tradesmen's formula suggests, however faintly, that the tradesmen know the Queen personally. That is vulgar enough. The phrase "to the Nation" diffuses the relationship and makes it unblushingly commercial, which is doubtless an improvement in moral terms; but in literary terms it is a disaster, and the implication that the freight is handled not by a freight agency but by a city—or by a big stormy man who throws it around—doesn't make much sense any way you look at it. The line is vulgar because it is false. That is to say, it is vulgar because of its content.

For style is partly a matter of content. Consider the statement with which the narrator of Thomas Mann's *Doctor Faustus* introduces himself: "My name is Serenus Zeitblom, Ph.D." On the first reading, its style seems to be due entirely to its content: without the initials "Ph.D." at the end, it would have no style at all; with them, it becomes delightful. Why does it delight us? Because it

gives us a signal to which we respond: it engages our imagination, and thereby—by means of the inferences we supply—reveals at once the pedantry of the narrator, the humor of the author, the detachment of author from narrator, and the equivocal tone and intention of the whole novel. By assuming that we can respond to the signal and supply all these things that are not explicitly given, it compliments our intelligence.

But such engagement would not be possible without the particular form of the content. If the narrator should introduce himself by saying, "My name is Serenus Zeitblom; I have a Ph.D.," the signal would be different, and weaker and inferior; it would not so deftly compliment our intelligence; the wit of Thomas Mann's formulation inheres in its form. The form, however, depends on the content—the precise content, the very words that Thomas Mann uses. For if the narrator should say, "I am Serenus Zeitblom, Ph.D.," his statement would lack the humor of the misstatement, "My name is Ph.D." It would also fail to reveal two other things it now reveals: the tension between Zeitblom's unconsciousness of his fatuity and Mann's consciousness of it, and the dramatic situation in which Mann stands between narrator and reader, manipulating one, glancing toward the other in expectation of understanding and good will. Thus, by his clever management of one sentence, Mann immediately identifies Dr. Zeitblom as a brother to Sancho Panza and Joyce's Shaun.

A good translation, I said, is good because of its literary qualities. I have quoted from H. T. Lowe-Porter's translation of *Doktor Faustus,* which in this sentence is literal and puts the words as nearly in the same order as the difference of the two languages will permit, the original being, "Mein Name ist Dr. Phil. Serenus Zeitblom." But since the idiomatic pattern of one language coincides only here and there with that of another, few sentences can be translated literally and even fewer word-for-word in the same order. Usually, as in this case, translating idiomatic German into idiomatic English requires a change of word order, if of nothing else; and when we change the word order we ask the reader to breathe differently. This shifts the emphases throughout the sentence. Serenus Zeitblom's next sentence, for example, reads thus in Mrs. Lowe-Porter's translation: "I deplore the extraordinary delay in introducing myself, but the literary nature of my material has prevented me from coming to the point until now." [6] A literal translation would read, "I myself deplore the strange postponement of this card-giving, but, as it has chanced and been ordained, the literary process of my communications would me until this moment ever not thereto come let." I don't think anyone would deny that Mrs. Lowe-Porter's version is better: she is a rather rare translator in that she knows her native language as well as the foreign one. The patterns of thought in different languages being so different, even the most literal translation, if it is not to be a parody, involves a restatement, a rearrangement, of the author's thought. Thus even an accurate carrying over of the ostensible content of simple prose can hardly preserve the tone and tune of the original; and it is notoriously all but impossible to preserve the tone and tune of poetry in translation.

The syntax of our thought necessarily depends on that of our language; and so do its manners, its bearing, step and demeanor. Can you imagine a French verse translation of *Paradise Lost* that would be anything at all like *Paradise Lost*? It would most probably have to be in rhyme, since the French custom of counting the silent *e*'s reduces the auditory interest of French verse to such an extent that without rhyme there would be very little indeed. (Try to imagine *The Canterbury Tales* without rhyme and you'll see what I mean.) Boileau's arguments in favor of rhyme (1674) seem to be a direct reply to Milton's arguments against it (1667), though they may very well not be; and if they are not, so much the better for my present thesis. On the one hand, Boileau didn't read English, and *Paradise Lost* wasn't translated into French until 1836; on the other hand, anyone who kept up with the literary news and gossip so assiduously as Boileau did was certainly aware of *Paradise Lost;* moreover, some of his remarks on how not to write an epic seem to be aimed at Milton as well as at Desmarets and Scudéri. But whatever the case may be, and although Milton was of course right for his own poem,

---

6. From *Doctor Faustus* by Thomas Mann. Copyright © 1947 by Thomas Mann. Copyright © 1948 by Alfred A. Knopf, Inc. Reprinted by permission of Alfred A. Knopf, Inc.

Boileau was right for French verse. So that it doesn't matter whether he was replying to Milton or not. For that 1836 translation—by Chateaubriand, no less—is in prose. In his preface Chateaubriand says it is only a kind of pony to help the reader read the great original, which he prints on the facing pages: "a literal translation . . . which a child as well as a poet can follow with the text, line for line, word for word, like a dictionary open before his eyes." He knows enough about the art of poetry, he says, not to presume to try for "une traduction *élégante*" (his italics). *Paradise Lost* in elegant French verse would be lost indeed. Consider, by way of illustration, the loss of Milton's sonnet on the Waldenses as translated by Valery Larbaud:

Venge, ô Seigneur, tes Saints égorgés, dont les os. . . .

The words are lexically accurate, but that waltzy rhythm is unjust both to Milton and to the Waldenses, who one would think had suffered enough.[7]

Of course not all verse translations of poetry are bad—not even all rhymed translations. One of Housman's few good poems is his translation of "Nous n'irons plus au bois"; Chaucer's translation of *Le Roman de la Rose* is at least as good as the original; and Milton's unrhymed lyric "What slender youth bedewed with liquid odours," translated from Horace, is worthy of Milton. But such achievements are extremely rare; more often, a good poet faced with a good poem in another language makes little or no effort to follow it faithfully: Yeats's "When you are old and grey and full of sleep" is not a translation but an original poem suggested by Ronsard's "Quand vous serez bien vieille, au soir à la chandelle," which was itself an original poem suggested by Tibullus' passage beginning "At tu casta maneas," so that there is no similarity at all between Yeats's poem and the corresponding part of Tibullus'.

As a rule, poetry translated by non-poets becomes non-poetry. It doesn't become prose. As far as literary value is concerned, it becomes nothing: for it has none. We may, to be sure, read it as

7. They were not, after all, Wienerwaldenses.

something other than literature: as a source of wisdom, perhaps, so
that we can write an essay on Man in the Cosmos or The Individual
and Society or Fate and Free Will: the same essay we wrote after
reading *Oedipus Rex,* and again after reading *Job,* and again after
reading *Hamlet,* and again, God spare us all, after reading *The Mayor
of Casterbridge.* How we miseducate the youth! Or we may read it as
a social datum or a bit of historical or biographical evidence or an
anthropological potsherd. As anything, in fact, but literature. The
same thing happens to prose when it is translated by a non-stylist or
an anti-stylist. Nobody reads Constance Garnett's translation of *The
Brothers Karamazov* as a novel. We all read it as philosophy or
morality or religion, or as a Picture of Russian Life in the Nineteenth
Century. We may, to be sure, have intended and in all good faith
started out to read it as a novel, but when we talk about it we always
talk about its moral or religious or psychological or political or social
or historical implications, never about its literary qualities: because
in Constance Garnett's language it has none. Likewise, we read
Herter Norton's almost inconceivably bad English version of *The
Notebooks of Malte Laurids Brigge* not as a masterpiece of literary
art but as an existentialist document and a source of Sartre's *Nausea*
and Weiss's *Exile.* On the other hand, even those of us who don't
subscribe to Saint Augustine's beliefs can enjoy the Pusey translation
of the *Confessions* as literature; and I find John Florio's unfaithful
version of Montaigne better reading than Donald Frame's faithful
one. In a sense, Florio was more faithful than Frame: for Montaigne
was not a great thinker like Norman Vincent Peale to whom we go
for wisdom but a highly readable writer to whom we go for pleasure.
We enjoy his conversation. We also enjoy Florio's personal reports of
it. I don't mean to imply that Frame is not excellent, but only that
he is not so hair-raisingly wonderful as Florio. Compare these two
versions of two consecutive sentences from the first essay, the first
version by Frame, the second by Florio:

> Edward, prince of Wales, the one who governed our Guienne so long (a
> person whose traits and fortune have in them many notable elements of
> greatness), having suffered much harm from the Limousins, and taking
> their city by force, could not be halted by the cries of the people and
> by the women and children abandoned to the butchery, who implored

his mercy and threw themselves at his feet—until, going farther and
farther into the city, he saw three French gentlemen who with
incredible boldness were holding out alone against the assault of his
victorious army. Consideration and respect for such remarkable valor
first took the edge off his anger, and he began with these three men to
show mercy to all the inhabitants of the city.[8]

*Edward* the black Prince of *Wales* (who so long governed our Country
of *Guienne,* a man whose conditions and fortune were accompanied
with many notable parts of worth and magnanimitie) having beene
grievously offended by the *Limousins,* though he by maine force took
and entred their Citie, could by no meanes be appeased, nor by the
wailefull out-cries of all sorts of people (as of men, women, and
children) be moved to any pitty, they prostrating themselves to the
common slaughter, crying for mercy, and humbly submitting themselves at his feet, untill such time as in triumphant manner passing
thorow their Citie, he perceived three French Gentlemen, who alone,
with an incredible and undaunted boldnesse, gainstood the enraged
violence, and made head against the furie of his victorious armie. The
consideration and respect of so notable a vertue, did first abate the dint
of his wrath, and from those three began to relent, and shew mercy to
all the other inhabitants of the said towne.

The difference between "the cries of the people" and "the
wailefull out-cries of all sorts of people" is the difference between
mere accuracy and literary genius. What I am saying is that a
translation can be a work of literary art; and that the peculiar
pleasure we take in a work of literary art depends on its quality as a
work of literary art and on our sensitivity to such quality. As C. S.
Lewis has observed, people who enjoy commonplace or inferior
writing enjoy it for other than literary reasons, and they are able to
enjoy it only because they are not sensitive to literary quality.
Kenneth Roberts fans enjoy Kenneth Roberts because they enjoy
looking for a northwest passage and fighting Indians; but we who
enjoy Samuel Beckett enjoy his language.

Does this mean that language is everything? Not quite. If language
were everything, such constructions as "I zigged when I shoulda
zagged" and "I boogied when I shoulda woogied," which do in fact

8. Reprinted with permission of the publisher from "By diverse means we
arrive at the same end," *The Complete Works of Montaigne,* translated by
Donald M. Frame (Stanford: Stanford University Press, 1957), p. 3.

THE CASE FOR IRRELEVANCE

give us a purely literary pleasure, would be better than the sentence
"In the beginning was the Word." The high quality of this sentence
is due not to its design but to the fact that it expresses perfectly an
idea which, whether we accept it or not, engages our intellect. We
may engage with the idea only in order to refute it, but it is a subtle
and difficult idea, and the perfect expression of it in that
syntactically simple sentence gives us a thrill of pleasure. If we try to
put it into the language of those who were educated by disciples of
John Dewey we can see how the quality of its substance depends on
the quality of its form: "Like first off there was . . . you
know . . . there was like this idea." Long's you know what I mean,
what differnt's make? The difference is the difference between
intellectual elegance and intellectual nose-picking: between a clear
mind and a mind too slack to formulate one clear sentence in its
native language. But of course that second sentence is a factitious
fake. I didn't hear it, I made it up. It would never occur in nature:
people who think in that idiom don't and can't have such thoughts.
A subtle idea can be artificially translated into muddled language,
but it could never come from a muddled mind. Fakery of this kind is
the basic weakness of many efforts to popularize difficult ideas, to
promote desirable points of view, and to express ideas that should be
taken seriously, through fiction that cannot be taken seriously.

Here, in the matter of literary judgment, we see the necessity of
distinguishing between the pleasures of art and the other pleasures
that art may suggest—including the pleasures of social anger and
political engagement. For many novels, stories, plays and poems that
one would think could not be taken seriously by anybody who
knows anything about the art are in fact taken seriously by many
people—critics, reviewers, teachers—who professionally profess to
know quite a bit about it. They do know quite a bit about it; and
nevertheless they take pleasure in books to take pleasure in which is
to be deluded. They are not insensitive to literary values; often they
have demonstrated a fine appreciation of nuances in works of the
past; but in their belief that literature should speak to the problems
of our time they tend to judge current fiction, drama and even
poetry by other than literary standards. When they enter the present
age they look for "relevance" above all: social relevance, political

relevance, ethical relevance: and when they find it their enthusiasm often leads them to mistake it for literary relevance. For the time being they forget that a work of art is good to the extent that it is relevant to itself, and that it need not necessarily be relevant to anything else at all.

In extreme cases they regard the literature of their own time in essentially the same way that a nutritionist or a health nut regards food: he doesn't care how it tastes as long as it's good for you—in fact, he suspects that if it tastes good it's bad for you: he lives on wheat germ, whey and iron filings, disapproves of anything that has to be cooked, and shrinks in moral disdain and physical horror from plum pudding. Many literary critics comport themselves toward the pleasures of contemporary literature with an equally aggressive moral rectitude. They have no use for "fine writing." They find Nabokov "precious" and Beckett "irrelevant." In their anti-dictatorial zeal—a zeal I share, let me remind you—they prefer *Darkness at Noon* and *1984* to *Pnin* and *How It Is.* These latter two, they will tell you, Take a Pessimistic View of Human Nature and Offer No Solutions to the Great Problems of Our Times. They will not say it of the former two. They regard with approval and even with perverse pleasure all kinds of commonplace or sub-common-place novels that attack racism or militarism or the TV industry or bigoted rural school boards, or that Dramatize the Need for Family Planning, or Reveal the Universal Pathos of the Human Condition in a Fascinating Byway of Medieval History, or Cast a Penetrating Light into Some of the Dark Corners of the Human Soul, or Blow the Lid Off the Dope Racket, or show how picturesque—i.e., good—is life in the dirt-road country of the northeast or southwest or northwest or southeast.

About such people not much can be done. The best course is to stay out of their way, and if possible keep our children out of their way, and observe three simple rules:

1. Read some verses of Thomas Campion every morning immed-iately on rising, and every evening immediately before retiring, to clear the blood.

2. Listen to a good record of Handel's *Acis and Galatea* once a week.

3. Faced with a new book, look at it, smell it, weigh it in your hand. If it doesn't look, smell and feel right, don't open it. If you open it, read the first paragraph aloud. If the rhythms are not pleasing, read no further. You won't be wrong.

# Social Relevance,
## Literary Judgment,
# and the
## New Right

Racial discrimination is a crime, whether or not the law says it is. It is a crime by nature, just as rape is a crime by nature, and for the same reason: it violates human personality. It insults the individual, and through him or her the species. It denies the fact that all human beings are equally human and equally entitled to be treated accordingly, with a decent regard for their feelings: not to be used as mere animals or inanimate objects. It is a violation of human nature and a crime against human nature.

Human nature also includes a capacity to produce and enjoy beautiful things: works of art: paintings, sculptures, architecture, music, literature; and to forbid us to take a disinterested non-utilitarian pleasure in them is also a violation of our nature, though of course not so serious as rape or racism. Often those who would have us enjoy works of art only for some ulterior purpose don't realize that they are going against a part of our nature; but they are. For a good work of art may or may not be an effective piece of propaganda, but we have a right to enjoy it whether it is or not; and an effective piece of propaganda may or may not be a good work of art, and if it isn't we have a right not to be pressured into saying that it is. As human beings, we have as much right not to be violated in our literary sensitivity as we have not to be raped or racially discriminated against. But in our propagandistic zeal for social justice we sometimes overlook this fact. We want literature to be relevant to our non-literary concerns—to have some propaganda value. This strategy seems to me crude, foolish and self-defeating; I am therefore going to make a few remarks in defense of literature whose only value is its high quality as literature.

Four well-known modern novels—Arthur Koestler's *Darkness at Noon,* George Orwell's *1984,* William Styron's *The Confessions of Nat Turner,* and Franz Kafka's *The Trial*—deal with men on trial for their lives; the first three of these novels have direct and obvious relevance to our current problems; but the fourth, which has little or no such relevance, is the only one with any literary value: the only one that is valuable in itself, for what it is: a work of art, a thing of beauty.

*Darkness at Noon,* which deals with the Moscow purge trials of the thirties, purports to explain how an intelligent man can be induced, partly by prolonged physical discomfort that amounts to torture by any but the most pedantically technical definition, and partly by appeals to a false patriotism, to confess a crime he didn't commit, in order to divert criticism from the leaders of the country. Whatever light it may throw on the Moscow purge trials, it has no radiance of its own. It is no diamond, it is a bag of mush. As a work of art, it doesn't exist. Whatever may be its career in the future as a political document, a testimony to the events of the thirties in Russia, it will never again be read for its own sake—if it ever was read for its own sake.

*1984* grows more relevant every day, as events increasingly show how prophetic Orwell's vision was. Every day, the world situation and the direction of our national life grow more crudely melo-dramatic, in the manner of the cheapest science fiction; and it becomes more apparent that *1984* is prophetic in proportion as it is crudely melodramatic cheap science fiction. It deals with the kind of things that happen only in real life and badly written books. This badly written book will doubtless live in English literary history as a

social novel or a political novel—as a bit of documentary evidence of
the life of our time—but it has never been enjoyed as a work of art,
and it never will be. As a work of art, it doesn't exist.

*The Confessions of Nat Turner* is a journalistic novel based on the
confession that Nat Turner was tricked into dictating to the
prosecuting attorney, who had said that he was the defense attorney,
and who moreover edited the confession to make it more damaging
and more conformable to the prejudices of the white-trash culture.
Styron's fictional version tries to recover the personality of Nat
Turner from under the attorney's rubbish, or to imagine and create a
personality in essentially the same way that Milton imagined and
created his heroic Satan. That Styron had some such grand intention
his inflated prose leaves no doubt; there can also be no doubt that he
succeeds in showing how and why a man may be driven to reject,
absolutely, totally, without reservation or distinction, the culture
that has robbed him of all human hope and insulted him from
morning to night every day of his life, even when it thought it was
being kind. To the extent that *The Confessions of Nat Turner* helps
us to understand the current black rejection of the white culture, it
is valuable. I will discuss this in some detail later. I will also show
why as a novel it is of no value at all—why as a work of art it doesn't
exist.

*The Trial* is the only one of the four novels that is a work of art.
It therefore has a different kind of relevance to our lives. Back in the
1940's, in an article in *Phylon*, L. D. Reddick said that black
intellectuals were unanimously enthusiastic about Kafka because
they found that he knew what their life was like. He knew what all
our lives are like. *The Trial* begins, "Someone must have traduced
Joseph K., for without having done anything wrong he was arrested
one fine morning." Joseph K. is an unexceptionably ordinary man, a
thirty-year-old bachelor who lives in a boarding house and works in a
bank. He is the chief clerk. He supervises all the other clerks and is
held responsible for the accuracy of their work. He takes pride in the
fact that he has a private office and two telephones—one for
interoffice calls and one for outside calls. He checks everything. He
is conscientious, efficient and thorough, all day, every day. The
manager likes him and occasionally invites him to dinner or

authorizes him to entertain a visiting customer at the bank's
expense. He has reason to believe that in time he will become
assistant manager and perhaps ultimately manager. His outside
phone doesn't connect him with any outside interests. He has no
interest in anything but his work and his chances of promotion. But
one fine morning, much to his surprise, he is arrested! Without
having done anything wrong! He is never informed of the charge,
and has no idea what it might be. His situation has the flat
verisimilitude and the uncomfortable implausibility of a rather dull
adult nightmare. He is not imprisoned. He continues to go to the
bank and do his work as usual, though now under great strain. At
night and on Sundays he asks questions of various people, but
nobody has any concrete information. He never gets to see the
judge. He is never asked to testify. He never hears anybody testify
against him. But there is no doubt that he is on trial. His lawyer tells
him his case is going badly. The court painter, whose job is to paint
flattering portraits of the judges, tells him that nobody has ever been
acquitted. A priest, who professes to be the prison chaplain, accosts
him in the cathedral one day and tells him that he is presumed to be
guilty because everybody is presumed to be guilty. He actually
begins to feel guilty, though not of anything in particular. And
finally, on the eve of his thirty-first birthday, two executioners come
to the boarding house and lead him out to an abandoned quarry and
stab him through the heart with a butcher knife. His last words are,
"Like a dog!"

Joseph K. dies like a dog because he has lived like a dog. He is
guilty of not having done anything wrong. He is guilty of never
having said, "No!" He is guilty of living a life of supine acquiescence.
He is guilty of being tame. He is guilty of being innocent.

The world is full of Joseph K.'s, and of the even more
commonplace acquiescent minds who work under them. That's why
it's in the state it's in. Most of the harm in the world is done not by
wicked people but by dull people. Most right-wingers are not
innately depraved: they are innately deprived, and culturally
depraved. Hitler, Nasser, George Wallace, Lester Maddox and their
millionaire backers are undoubtedly wicked, but when we look at
the upturned faces of their poor followers what we see is not so

much wickedness as ignorance and stupidity. Fortunately, the gradual raising of the educational level in this country has so reduced the numbers of the ignorant and stupid that no undisguised rightist now has enough followers to carry more than four or five states out of fifty. That's why the right hates intellectuals; that's why it hates to see public money spent for liberal education, and that's why the cleverer rightists now call themselves pragmatists or even leftists. Nixon calls himself a pragmatist. Nasser calls himself a leftist. The fact that Nixon doesn't dare go as far to the right as Nasser reflects the higher literacy rate and the generally higher level of education in the United States. Americans, by and large, are better informed than Egyptians. We are therefore harder to fool.

We are harder to fool not because we have more technical training but because we have more of the critical, skeptical, humorous intelligence that comes with liberal education. American military etiquette doesn't go so far as heel-clicking, because American civilians would laugh at it, and would not tolerate the authoritarian arrogance of which it is a symbol.

I therefore believe in the development of a critical, skeptical, humorous habit of mind—in the development of a liberally educated consciousness, a sensitivity to nuances and unstated implications, an ability to read between the lines and to hear undertones and overtones—both for the sake of political and social enlightenment and for the sake of our personal enlightenment and pleasure as individuals. I am a teacher of literature and of writing because I believe that precision, clarity, beauty and force in the use of language, and appreciative perception of these qualities in the language of others, not only make us harder to fool but are good things in themselves; since in a free society we are not only citizens but also individuals—since we live not primarily for the state but for ourselves and our friends and loved ones—I believe that the cultivation and refinement of our tastes—in literature, in music, in painting and sculpture and architecture, in eating and drinking, in sex, in love, in all our human responses and relations—is a good in itself; I believe that the more sensitively we perceive things the more fully we can live and the less likely we are to be imposed on by advertisers, politicians and other saviors. I must therefore defend those of us who try to cultivate literary sensitivity in the young, against those who preach that in our present situation such sensitivity is irrelevant. It is not we who are anti-democratic; it is those who would blunt the perceptions of the rising generation—whether with drugs or with flatulent oratory or with bad art—who are consciously or unconsciously anti-democratic.

In our time the struggle is no longer between right and left but between right and right: between the old anti-Communist right, represented by such as George Wallace, William Buckley, Jr., Lester Maddox, John Wayne, Ronald Reagan, Richard Daley, Hubert Humphrey, Lyndon Johnson, Strom Thurmond, and Richard Nixon, and the new pro-Communist right, represented by men of equal crudity, who consciously or unconsciously serve Moscow's rightist foreign policy—its support of whatever dictatorships and monarchies seek its support, and its opposition to all liberal régimes—with as much fervor as the American Communist Party supported Nazism during the period of the Hitler-Stalin pact: I mean specifically the anti-Semitic Leslie Campbell, Eldridge Cleaver, LeRoi Jones, Rap Brown, Stokely Carmichael and Sonny Carson. The old right has always resisted the spread of education and has been steadily pushed back by the forces of liberal decency; now the new right is trying to destroy the universities—especially those that admit black students in more than token numbers. The new segregationists and the new Uncle Toms call themselves radicals—and no doubt many of them sincerely believe they are radicals; nevertheless, in their unskeptical zeal they are ignorantly doing the work of the John Birch Society. The old right has always promoted racial and religious prejudice, and has only recently begun to show signs of wishing to avoid the contempt of decent liberals; now the new right is coming to its aid with open appeals to racial and religious prejudice. The old right has always discouraged clear and independent thinking by the young, and it still tries to cajole its own sons and daughters into conformity with the brand-name culture; now it is urging those of us who are not cajolable to blow our minds; and the new right has joined forces with such old rightists as Marshall McLuhan, Hugh Kenner, Norman Brown, Tim Leary and the Beatles in urging us to feel more and think less—to relax, to drop out, to avoid logic, to give ourselves up to indiscriminate unanalyzed sensation until we are no longer able to (you know) say clearly like what we mean or even to (you know) like *know* what the fuck we mean. That is the classic technique of fascism: blow their minds with ritual and rhythmic chanting and drugs, and they'll follow you anywhere. There's nothing new about it. Not to go all the way back to the Bacchae, back in the 1940's the late Aldous Huxley, who believed that education should be limited to the hereditary upper classes, was preaching the joys of chemically induced mystical states—that is, of cheap, effortless, brainless, instant mysticism for the masses; and in the 1920's that fascist sympathizer D. H. Lawrence was saying that workers should wear red pants and dance in the sun instead of organizing and demanding a larger share of what they produce. Such irresponsible flim-flam, flapdoodle, silly-juice and happy-dust are standard mind-paralyzers used by all contemporary dictatorships. For there are no leftist dictatorships now; in the modern world, all dictatorships are of the right; the difference between such countries as the United States and England with all their bourgeois democratic sins on the one hand, and Russia, China, Greece, Cuba, Spain, Portugal and Egypt with all their authoritarian virtue on the other, is that in each of the bourgeois democracies there are many voices saying many different things but in each of the dictatorships there is only one voice. The present intellectual tone of the American government is to be sure a monotone, that of *The Reader's Digest,* Norman Vincent Peale, Billy Graham, Lawrence Welk and J. Edgar Hoover; nevertheless, in my classroom at an American university I introduce the students to other voices, the avant-garde voices of Samuel Beckett, Alain Robbe-Grillet, Michel Butor, Jorge Luis Borges, Tommaso Landolfi, Heinrich Böll and Günter Grass—all of them foreigners, not one of them a nice boy—and nobody tells me not to. But we know what happens to avant-garde writers in Russia, China, Greece and Spain; and what do you think would happen to a professor of English at Moscow University if he told his students the sad truth that the apolitical Henry James wrote better novels than the Socialist Jack London, or that Edgar Allan Poe, who believed in slavery, was a somewhat better poet then John Greenleaf Whittier, who fought against it, or that the best American poet of the twentieth century was alas not a man of the people named Carl Sandburg but a reactionary insurance man named Wallace Stevens? The imperial United States, to be sure, has its CIA infiltrating and sabotaging liberal movements in other countries; and imperial Communist Russia and China undoubtedly have their infiltrators sabotaging liberal American universities. Their clichés are unmistakable. There's nothing avant-garde about *them.* Mao tse-Tung is the Norman Vincent Graham of the Communist world. The corn is as high as an elephant's eye.

If we are to preserve the right to express different views, we must preserve and cultivate the rare ability to have different views—the ability to think independently. We must not accept rides from strangers: we must not take a trip to lotus-land on that yellow submarine the LSD, whose call letters, incidentally, stand for pounds, shillings and pence. We must learn the old half-lost techniques of reading, word by word, line by linear line, understanding and silently conversing with the author, working out our own thoughts in partial agreement or complete disagreement with his. As we read we must test every sentence, not only for its ostensible meaning but also for its incidental and perhaps unintended implications—its tone. In (you should pardon the expression) *The New York Times Book Review* for February 2, 1969, Adam Walinsky says of Daniel P. Moynihan's book *Maximum Feasible Misunderstanding: Community Action in the War on Poverty,*

> This is *not* the slashing, all-out attack on the community-action program that the press and some excerpts have led us to expect. . . . What is distressing is the tone of the book: basically anti-intellectual, anti-participatory, quietist, above all flattering of that very political passivity which we may now, I suppose, expect to be the domestic keynote of Mr. Moynihan's new Administration. What he is telling us, most clearly, is that we should study more and do less. Against this tone, against the complacency it encourages, his defenses of community action are small beer indeed; and basically ineffectual, since, like so much else in the book, they are pure assertion.

Then, after analyzing the ostensible substance of the book in some detail, Mr. Walinsky returns, as he says, "to the central question of tone. I hope I am wrong, but what this book seems to be is a long exercise in condescension: to Government officials, to social thinkers, above all to the poor themselves." [1] Mr. Walinsky writes well because he reads well. He is aware, much more than Mr. Moynihan himself, of the literary quality of Mr. Moynihan's prose. He has a very keen literary sensitivity. We who try to help our students develop such sensitivity can do it best by working with technical niceties of many kinds, through the whole range of literary forms, genres and movements; such minute concerns may very well seem irrelevant to those who have never been concerned with them, and doubtless they find our whole enterprise irrelevant; but they are wrong, and those of us who yield to their crude dissuasions do so because we suffer from a false and unwarrantable sense of guilt.

Anyone who reads J. L. and Barbara Hammond's *The Bleak Age* or Henry Mayhew's *London Labour and the London Poor* must recognize that poverty was more widespread, more degrading and more hopeless in Victorian England than in modern England; and anyone who has any acquaintance with the history of the American labor movement knows that poverty in America was more widespread, more degrading and more hopeless in the late nineteenth and early twentieth centuries than it is now. Moreover, militarism, racism, religious bigotry, political corruption and police brutality in both countries were even worse than they are now, and the problems of health and education were much more serious and got much less attention. But with the spread of literacy, the diffusion of newspapers and magazines and books, and the invention of radio and television, large numbers of people have emerged from the helpless condition of being totally uninformed and totally voiceless; as they have slowly gained information and articulacy, the suffrage has ineluctably followed; beyond the suffrage, they are now beginning to take part in the continuing public discussion that goes on between elections; therefore neither government nor the established organs and institutions of the traditional culture can any longer ignore their needs, their feelings, their self-respect.

---

In the unaccustomed process of not ignoring them, our official spokesmen often find it politic or convenient to suggest that the traditional culture is the enemy of the people. For their purposes, intellectuals, whose idiom, interests, tastes, ritual gestures and pious observances differ from those of the Hooper-rated majority, are roughly analogous to Negroes, Jews and foreigners: the wrath of the frustrated can easily be turned against them and thereby diverted from the real causes of frustration. In the election of 1968 George Wallace got most of the white-trash vote by attacking intellectuals, and both major parties were careful to nominate candidates who could not by any stretching of language be accused of intellectual distinction. People who bear the marks of disinterested intelligence are too different from our standard-brand politicians to get the Good Housekeeping Seal of Approval. We academics are considered to be cold, aloof, snobbish, out of touch with and indifferent to the interests, problems and sufferings of the majority.

Theoretically, we should all feel guilty, the way Joseph K. felt guilty; happily, most of us don't. We have only contempt for the easy tears of Schopenhauer, whose self-indulgent grieving over the oppressed plebeians of ancient Rome didn't prevent his being coldly cruel in his daily life. In a well-known book he professed to suffer all the injustices of the past through a compassionate identification with their victims. But when the poor old woman who cleaned up his bachelor apartment disturbed him while he was writing one afternoon, he kicked her downstairs and broke her hip. Since he was rich, an exceptionally liberal court ordered him to pay the old woman, for the rest of her life, as much as she had been earning from all her cleaning jobs. A few years later she died, and when Schopenhauer heard the news he wrote in his diary, "Obit anus, abit onus"—"The old woman is dead, the burden is lifted." The wit of his Latin evaporates in translation, but the vileness of his heart comes through with undiminished stench. So much for the value of his philosophy of compassion. If our compassion for the victims of injustice in the past doesn't affect our behavior in the present, it is a phony emotion; and since we can do nothing about past injustices, to feel guilty of them is a vain, fatuous and self-indulgent waste of time. Nobody in this room is guilty of the Saint Bartholomew's Day massacre of 1572, for example, or the hanging of little children accused of theft in the eighteenth century, or the whipping of Quakers in colonial Massachusetts, or the slavery that separated black families and violated their humanity until 1865, or the establishment of the Ku Klux Klan to resume the violation after 1865, or the starvation that is now killing and stunting people in Africa, India, Latin America and the Southern United States, or the slums that ruin people's lives in cities everywhere. Nobody in this room is guilty of any of these things, I say, and to reproach ourselves for them is to confuse our thinking and divert emotional energy that could be better spent on the problems at hand. Many of us academics, who instead of weeping useless tears over past injustices work for the correction of present injustices, are accustomed to being sneered at by conservatives, who call us "bleeding hearts," and I suppose we will have to become accustomed to being sneered at by the new allies of conservatism, who call us "racist bastards." We work for the correction of present injustices even though we are not personally to blame for them and should not properly feel guilty about them. We realize moreover that we have not only the right but the duty to do our own academic work, even if it has nothing to do with the correction of injustice or the relief of suffering. For it is valuable in other ways, which are equally human.

But we in the traditional liberal arts have a special problem; so that even though we don't feel guilty of crimes we didn't commit, many of our students feel guilty for us. Nobody criticizes a physicist who spends most or all of his time studying and teaching physics, but many people criticize us who spend most or all of our time studying and teaching literature. Nobody doubts the importance of the natural sciences, because their objectivity, their precision and their detailed concreteness do demonstrably increase our knowledge of the natural world, and their applications have brought about both ameliorations of human life that gratify our sense of our own and others' worth, and spectacular devastations that gratify our sense of our own and others' depravity. Nobody doubts the importance of the social sciences, because they do replace our superstitions about the human world with facts that can be used in gratifying both these senses. Nobody doubts the importance of the abstract sciences of mathematics and logic, because they provide useful tools for natural and social scientists. And some few of us go so far as to recognize the intrinsic value of the aesthetic gratification that abstract scientists, social scientists and natural scientists alike experience in playing with concepts. This gratification is somehow connected in our vague apprehension with a vague something we call "the mystery of nature," to which we too respond with sympathetic vibrations. We recognize the human value of the sciences.

But literature is not a science; few people recognize its value, and many even of those few question its importance. Even some of those who are professionally engaged in studying and teaching it often wonder whether they are doing anything worth doing; they are tempted to use their professional work as a means of becoming engaged in something else, something that seems to them more significant: moral exhortation, social protest, political action: and if they yield to the temptation they tend to evaluate writers by the scale of moral earnestness or social concern or political commitment rather than by the scale of literary competence. That is a disastrous mistake. It makes it impossible for them to help students develop a sensitivity to language that will enable them to tell good writing from bad, good arguments from phony arguments, valid emotion from weepy Schopenhauerisches schmaltz or Norman Vincent Peale commercial religiosity or John Wayne sadistic patriotism. A person who values Lillian Smith, Pearl Buck, John Steinbeck and William Styron as writers because of their liberalism is on no firmer ground than one who values Ayn Rand, Graham Greene, Aldous Huxley and Dorothy Sayers as writers because of their conservatism. Corn is corn, and liberal corn is no better than conservative corn. Likewise condescension is condescension, and at least in terms of literary quality liberal condescension is no better than conservative con- descension. These liberal cornballs are undoubtedly unaware of their corndescension. They don't mean to corndescend. But we think in words; to the extent that we recognize our feelings we even feel in words, and these writers have such a weak command of language that they have little command of their thoughts or even of their feelings. What comes out is something they don't intend, but since they don't hear how ridiculous it sounds they think they do intend it. Thus with the best of conscious intentions they unintentionally give themselves away.

Rousseau is a prize example of those writers who don't know what they are saying. We read his works not because they have any great intrinsic value but because he got around a great deal and knew many people and was a witness to the life of his time—so that his works are valuable to students of intellectual and social history in essentially the same way that the records of a shipping company would be valuable to a student of economic history.

In *Musings of a Solitary Walker,* for example, he recalls how distressed he was by one of the "low pleasures" of some rich friends he visited in 1757. He went with them to a village fair:

> Squares of gingerbread were on sale, and it occurred to one of the young men to buy some and throw them one by one into the crowd; my friends took so much pleasure in seeing those clodhoppers running, scuffling and knocking each other down in order to get some, that they all began to imitate the young man, and squares of gingerbread went flying right and left, and laborers male and female were running, jostling, brawling, fighting and maiming each other. All my friends found it charming.

Having indicated his disapproval in advance, Rousseau is on firm ground thus far. But Rousseau is never on firm ground for long. Sooner or later his solitary walks always lead him into a quaking bog of sentimentality, and he sinks over head and ears in it, bubbling with pleasure as perverse as that of his rich friends. For (as we have seen in the case of Schopenhauer) sentimentality is the very opposite of moral sensitivity, just as it is the opposite of aesthetic sensitivity; and the most remarkable feature of Rousseau's *Musings* is the blundering naiveté with which he reveals the coarseness of his own perceptions. As he proceeds in his account of the amusements at the fair, we are disappointed to discover that the one he most enjoys is one that gives him, like his friends, the crude pleasure of dramatizing his economic superiority. At first, he says, he joined the others in throwing gingerbread because he would have been embarrassed not to, although "inwardly" he was "less amused than they":

But soon, annoyed at squandering my money in order to degrade people, I left that jolly company and wandered alone through the fair. The variety of sights amused me for a long time. I saw among others five or six little chimney-sweeps around a little girl who still had in her stall a dozen wretched apples she would have been glad to get rid of. The chimney-sweeps for their part would have been glad to rid her of them, but they had only two or three *liards* among them [a *liard* being worth about half a cent], and that was not enough to make any great breach among the apples. That stall was for them the garden of the Hesperides, and the little girl was the dragon guarding it. This comedy amused me for a long time; I brought it to an end by paying the little girl for the apples and having her distribute them to the little boys. I then enjoyed one of the sweetest sights that can gratify the heart of man, that of joy united with the innocence of childhood spreading all around me, for those who saw it also shared in it; and I, who at such small expense also shared that joy, had the additional joy of knowing that it was brought about by me.

Comparing this amusement with those I had just left, I felt with satisfaction how different are wholesome tastes and natural pleasures from those born of opulence, which are almost nothing but those of mockery and the exclusivism engendered by scorn.

Though Rousseau's predominant feeling here is one of self-satisfaction in his moral superiority, he is not so far superior to his rich friends as he thinks; for the sentimental pleasure of his self-conscious benevolence, though undoubtedly superior to the brutal pleasures of his unself-conscious friends, depends like theirs on taking a superior position. In this episode as in many others, he condescends. For all his self-absorption, he has little self-knowledge; his psychology is thin and superficial. Proust gives us deep psychological insights; Rousseau doesn't.

Nor is Rousseau's language worth reading for the sake of its quality as language. In fact, it is sprinkled with ineptitudes of the kind we correct in freshman themes. In the brief passage about the village fair, for example, the sentence I translated, "But soon, annoyed at squandering my money in order to degrade people," etc., reads literally, "But soon, annoyed at emptying my purse in order to degrade people," etc. This way of putting it suggests the misleading interpretation that Rousseau didn't find the game intolerable until his purse was empty; it therefore gives us pause a few lines later, when the incident of the chimney-sweeps and the apples reveals that his purse was not empty after all. This is bad writing. It is clumsy writing. The essay in which it appears has no literary value at all. It might very well be used as illustrative material by a teacher of social history or social psychology; its usefulness for their purposes is obvious; but if an English teacher, impressed by its social relevance, should present it to his students as a model of good writing, he would be neglecting their education.

That is just what has to be said about Styron's *The Confessions of Nat Turner:* that the appearance of such a novel at this time is an interesting social fact, that the novel itself can help us to understand why many Negroes totally reject all the values of the society in which they live and are not impressed by white liberalism, and that it can therefore be useful to sociologists and political scientists who discuss current problems in their classes; but that it is very badly written, that therefore it is one of those books that enter into literary history without being discussable as literature, merely by virtue of the fact that they appeared and were widely read—books such as *Uncle Tom's Cabin* and *Main Street;* that English teachers who discuss it as literature don't know what they are doing, and that those who use it as a source of ideas for freshman themes would do better to use a book that is itself well written.

*The Confessions of Nat Turner* is not well written. It is very sloppily written. Styron's choice of words is often inaccurate, his ear for the realities of speech is unreliable, his handling of metaphors is frequently ludicrous, and sometimes he is even ungrammatical. Here are a few examples of his heavy infelicity, chosen pretty much at random from among so many others that to list them all would be boring.[2] Though there are no titles of nobility in America, Styron speaks of a Virginia plantation's "titled owner," meaning its titular owner. Sometimes he uses British words, such as "greatcoat" for overcoat and "hard by" for close to or near. He says, "Fleet as a deer, Hark scampered across the open lot, bare black feet sowing

---

2. All quotations are from *The Confessions of Nat Turner* by William Styron, copyright © 1966 by Random House, Inc. Reprinted by permission of Random House, Inc.

puffs of dust." Of course he means raising or kicking up puffs of dust, not sowing them; but a more serious mistake in this sentence is the word "scampered." To scamper is to run away from danger, as out of the path of a runaway horse, or to run playfully about like a child; to call the normal running of a grown man scampering is to be contemptuous, however unconsciously. Styron even has Nat Turner call a big strong Negro a "buck"—a word that would never under any circumstances be used by anyone so keenly conscious of outraged black dignity as Turner. Styron is unintentionally condescending because he has a very weak and uncertain command of language. He describes a poor white counting dollar bills with a "wettened" finger, meaning a wetted finger. He makes Turner speak of his new owner's "desire for my domination," meaning his "desire to dominate me." He makes Turner say, "I was further soothed by a fly's insensate deafening mutter as it settled on the topmost edge of my ear." Flies don't mutter, they buzz; and even in an empty room the buzzing of a fly would not be deafening. Styron speaks of "titanic lightning bolts," though the titans were defeated by Zeus because he had lightning bolts and they didn't. He tells how a neurotic poor white whom Turner had baptized emerged from the water and "stood there dripping and puffing like a kettle." Have you ever seen a kettle dripping and puffing? Kettles don't puff, anyhow; steam engines puff. He says that after a sleet storm "the countryside was sheathed in a glistening, crystalline coverlet of ice." Grease and oil, being soft, glisten; ice, being hard, glitters. And a coverlet is a kind of bedspread, not a sheath of ice on a tree. Styron has poor Negroes and poor whites alike use the standard English word "food" instead of "vittles" or "grub," which are the words they did and do use. He makes slaves in the early nineteenth century use such late-twentieth-century slang expressions as "he gib me a bad time" and "he smell up a storm." He says "could not but help" for "could not help but," "as if it was" for "as if it were," "presently" for "at present," "begat" for "begotten," and "yet even more importantly" for "but even more important." He makes Turner say, "Many of the Negroes paid scant interest to what I had to say"—not "paid scant attention to" or "took scant interest in" but "paid scant interest to." He makes Turner say, "I had become drenched in sweat and the droplets swarmed in my eyes." I suppose we should be thankful that he didn't say they swarmed like muttering flies. And how's this for a description of a farm?—"A gross hairless man with a swinish squint to his eyes, his farm lay several miles to the northeast of Moore's." If that doesn't say the farm was a gross hairless man, then no English sentence says anything. When Turner speaks of the pure implacable hatred that some Negroes feel toward all whites, Styron makes him say, "Like a flower of granite with cruel leaves, it grows, when it grows at all, as if from fragile seed cast upon uncertain ground." A flower of granite may very well be carved on a tombstone or a building, but how does it grow? And what are cruel leaves? And if a flower grows in a piece of ground, what is the meaning of the statement that the ground is uncertain? Sometimes Styron says just the opposite of what he means. At a time when there was a seller's market in slaves, he has Turner say, "Half a dozen traders were snooping around all over the county, and although I myself was doubtless safe I could not say that I felt the same about the other slaves I knew—including those present—and feared that only a clock-tick and some owner's necessity or greed might separate any of them from Mississippi or Arkansas." This says that an owner's necessity or greed might keep him from selling a slave to a trader who offered a high price, but the whole context indicates that Styron meant to say that an owner's necessity or greed might lead him to sell—an eventuality that Turner himself had experienced more than once. Finally, here are two metaphors involving horses. Styron makes Turner say, "I prodded the horse on with a snap of the reins," though the motion of prodding and the motion of snapping the reins are quite different; by the time the reader sees that he is supposed to take the word "prodded" metaphorically, he has already taken it literally; he then stops and mentally rewrites the sentence to read, "I urged the horse on with a snap of the reins," and concludes that Styron has once again been inept. I will not rewrite but leave in its original glory one last ineptitude: Styron says a farmer ordered a slave to saddle up a fat gelding and then "climbed aboard his bovine steed." As far as I know, that's the only horse in literature that looks like an ox.

All these infelicities and many others notwithstanding, *The*

*Confessions of Nat Turner* does show how a man whose humanity has been implicitly denied and explicitly violated all his life may very well reject all the values of the society that has so insulted him. It can therefore be profitably discussed in college courses concerned with social and political problems. But no novel so sloppily written can be called a work of art or profitably discussed as a work of art. *The Confessions of Nat Turner* has no place in any college course concerned with literature or with writing.

Literary sensitivity and moral sensitivity should ideally go together, but in fact they often don't. We think of Yeats, Pound, Eliot, Roy Campbell, the anti-Dreyfusard Paul Valéry, the Confederate sympathizers John Crowe Ransom and Allen Tate, and the Nazi sympathizers Paul Claudel and Louis-Ferdinand Céline—all good writers, all (at least by implication) defenders of kidnapping, rape, torture and murder. They were all miseducated. That is the intellectual tragedy of our age. But we cannot improve the education of future novelists and poets by presenting to them as models to emulate sloppy writers who are all heart and no brain.

The problem is not insoluble, however: for though it is true that not all good writers have good hearts, it is equally true that many of them do; and some of their works, which are among the supreme literary masterpieces not only of our time but of all time, can profitably be studied not only for their literary qualities but for their social, political and moral implications as well. I think of *Remembrance of Things Past, The Castle, The Trial, The Tin Drum* and *Ulysses,* whose technical sophistication, warm humanity and clear perception of the modern world make them suitable for all our purposes.

# Our
# Linguistic
# Servility

Macaulay quotes a classicist to the effect that Milton's mistakes in Latin are such as are due to the carelessness of a native rather than to the unfamiliarity of a foreigner. But we who struggle to teach natives born to the English language to speak and write it accurately are up against something trickier than carelessness and more systematic than unfamiliarity.

There is of course the common phenomenon of a native's unfamiliarity with the standard forms of his native language, which are not used in his family or his milieu: all we English teachers have had in our classes descendants of families who have been speaking English sloppily since 1066 or 597; but these, I suggest, are only a subgroup in a much larger class of the linguistically disabled: those who subconsciously choose to miss the target.

A person who says "accidently" and "incidently" will always say "evidentally"; he will say "assept" but "excape"; he will pronounce *league* "lig," *clique* "click" and *creek* "crick," but *handkerchief* "handkercheef"; he will say "athaletic" and "fillum," but "histry" and "mystry," and will reduce *delivery* to "livry" and *infirmary* to

"firmry"; he will say "esculator" and "perculator," but "insalation,"
"calclator" and "reglator"; he gasses up his car with Snoco, but his
wife polishes her nails with Revalon; in the same sentence in which
he observes that a girl tracks a lot of attention he will spress the
hope that there won't nobody attackt her like they tackted that
there other girl that was so poplar; after a trip to Washington he will
tell you that he visited the Spreme Court and when he come out it
was rainin and he didn't have no umberella, and ever since then he's
been suffrin from tonslitis and artheritis; for him, the state of
Emerson and Thoreau is Masschusetts but the rubber center of the
world is Acheron, Ohio; if he is a radio or TV announcer, he will
carelessly say "Noo York" and carefully say "afternune"; if he is a
hunter, he will tell you that the lass time he went huntn he worn
some new boots an they was so stiff he got all wore out; and when
he sits down to write, the same fatality that makes him write
"seperate" also makes him write "desparate." The fact that he sees
the correct spellings and hears the correct pronunciations every day
is of no avail. He has a deep neurotic need to be wrong: to speak a
language in which it is impossible to think very clearly. This is not
rebellion, this is servility.

Let us now approach the problem from a widely different angle
of vision, and then from a third, somewhat closer to the first; I
believe that the three approaches, though they will not of themselves
enable us to solve the problem, will enable us to see somewhat more
clearly what it is and what a solution will require.

In the fourth chapter of *Orlando,* Virginia Woolf takes us to an
eighteenth-century assembly in the drawing room of Lady R. The
conversation is quite ordinary, but all the guests are enchanted with
their own and each other's wit; then Mr. Pope arrives, makes three
witty remarks, dispels the spell and spoils the party. "One such
saying was bad enough," says Mrs. Woolf; "but three, one after
another, on the same evening! No society could survive it."

No society could survive it. Not only no society in the sense in
which society editors use the term, but no society in the sense in
which anthropologists and sociologists use it. For there is no game if
we don't observe the rules, and in order for society to survive, our
behavior must be predictable. To the extent that we are social

beings, we must do and say what everybody else does and says: the
regular things, the unexceptional and unexceptionable things, the
orthodox things, the ordinary things. But wit is by nature
exceptional and unexpected, and as social beings we enjoy it only to
the extent that it is harmless after all, that it raises no questions that
have not already occurred to us. When we joke about things that we
still take seriously, we are careful to do so in a way that leaves no
doubt that we are "only joking"—with a gentleman's light self-
deprecation or an entertainer's servile presumption, a trick that
makes us laugh at him rather than at the ostensible object of his
mockery. Wit goes through the motions of destruction, but if it is
really destructive we are either shocked or grimly pleased, not
amused. To be unequivocally free and original, however wittily, is to
be no longer harmless. Unmitigated originality is always bad form.
"The switch," said Bergson, "follows for a time the rail it is leaving";
and even so, the change of direction involves some loss of
smoothness at what engineers call the point of tangency. All change
is uncomfortable; all originality is suspect; all deviation from the
standard, whether downward or upward, is liable to social disapproval; and the standard is whatever is expected of us in the social
group in which we move and in the larger society that includes all
social groups.

But beyond social approval, many of us feel a need for divine
approval. Bear with me; suspend your disbelief for a while; for this
brings us to our third angle of vision. Between the incidently-evi-
dentally linguistic pervert and Alexander Pope stands a man of
ordinary or perhaps something more than ordinary sensitivity to
language: a college English major. Speaking and writing, he would
gladly utter things of the kind that Mrs. Woolf said spoiled the
party: things of "true wit, true wisdom, true profundity." In a
college theme or term paper there is no question of spoiling the
party: he knows that wit, wisdom and profundity will be warmly
appreciated. And nevertheless, from a deep fear—fear, I think, not of
social disapproval but of divine disapproval—he writes sentences
which, though not ungrammatical, are meaningless. He writes, "The
introduction of the actual object added the dimension of reality
which was the implicit reality of the object itself." He writes, "Stress

is placed upon the sequence of events and the investigative detail of scenic descriptions." He writes, "Man's union with the divine is the bringing forth of creativity to the greatest extent, although the resulting code may not be explicit in its visibility while very tight in its behavior." He writes, "For Sartre emotion is one mode of an attempt to achieve self-identity which is a motivational explanation for human behavior." He writes, "All external events which precede the novel are as meaningless and eventful as those of the internal kind are to the total gesture." He writes, "Hawkes' style contains that awareness of form which refers to effects, while evoking the threads of narrative continuity." He writes, "Joyce is much more organizational than earlier critics had given him reason to be." What the unsophisticated linguistic pervert does vis-à-vis society, the college English major does vis-à-vis whatever idea of transcendent reality he subconsciously fears: he demonstrates that he is harmless, that he has no intention of rising even into intelligibility, much less into originality. Only God is allowed to be creative.

But of course the fear of God and the fear of society are not absolutely separate and distinct. By the use of sentences that hover at the threshold of intelligibility without quite crossing it, the college English major undoes the effect on his human audience of his careful footnotes, his annotated bibliography and all his other apparatus of intellectuality: he assures the guardians of the social order that—although he is indeed an intellectual—he is not dangerous. Innocent muddle-headedness is not held to be socially dangerous, and neither is originality unless it is stated so clearly as to seem intelligible to large numbers of people. Professionals will accept a new idea if they see that it is useful, and laymen will accept it if they don't think they understand it. My physicist friends tell me that Einstein's originality was accepted by physicists because it resolved inconsistencies that were troubling them and answered questions they were asking; and it was accepted by the general public because it was mysterious and seemed unintelligible. But Darwin's and Freud's ideas had a much rougher time, even among biologists and psychologists, because their social implications were immediately apparent; and in some rural areas to this very day they are not accepted by local school boards and other guardians of the popular mysteries, because their implications seem clear even to those who have not read the books in which they are set forth. Scopes was a small-town teacher of rare courage.

We have it on the very best authority that innocence is incompatible with the knowledge of good and evil; and the story of the Tower of Babel seems to extend the ban on moral insight to intellectual clarity as well—if indeed they were ever separable. It was perhaps inevitable that Lucifer, the Light-Bearer, should become Satan, the Enemy. The struggle between the Enemy and the Community of Saints is the basic conflict in all human affairs; and if the best of the argument is with those who seek knowledge and inner development, the weight of feeling is with those who oppose it. Language itself, the peculiar expression of humanity, expresses the weight of anti-human feeling. The verb "glose," which originally meant to explain, now means to explain away or deceive; such words as "crafty," "cunning," "wily," "sharp," "smart," "subtle," "knowing," "artful" and "sophisticated" have undergone a similar moral deterioration, while "simple," "unsophisticated," "artless" and "naive" have become synonyms for "innocent." Intellectuals themselves use "innocent" as a synonym for "ignorant" and "unskillful," as in the sentences "He is innocent of grammar" and "He is innocent of style." "Be good, sweet maid, and let who will be clever," we say. "She's a nice, unsophisticated girl," we say; we hope she will marry a gentleman, not a "wise" guy. "Don't get wise wid me," says the policeman. In *Finnegans Wake* the fluff-headed Leapyear Girls address their favorite teacher, the good Shaun, who advises them to read "sifted science" and "pious fiction," as "Pattern of our unschoold"—of our *Unschuld*, our guiltlessness, our innocence. My German dictionary tells me that *klug* means clever and *Klügelei* means chicanery; my French dictionary tells me that *habile* means clever and deceitful, and *malin* means sly and clever. We can be diabolically but not angelically clever. We can be fiendishly but not angelically ingenious. Even among the ancient Greeks, *sophos* meant both wise and corrupt, and *chrestos* meant both good and simple-minded. To teach the youth to think clearly is, according to the deepest instinct of our natural or folk wisdom, to corrupt them. Prometheus was punished only incidentally for teaching men the use of fire, but primarily for teaching them to reason; and Laocoön and Cassandra were both punished for seeing too clearly. We play it safe by professing to find nature more reasonable than reason. Consider Swift's clean Houyhnhnms and dirty scientists. Consider all the noble savages and natural men who inhabit our literary woods and sail our symbolic seas. These clean, good, wholesome children of nature are phantoms who haunt our students, leading undergraduates into incoherence and graduates into quasi-learned babbling.

The nature of the disorder being what it is, we must attack it at the source, not in the symptoms. Knowledge of the rules of grammar is no help at all to a mind so haunted. We all know people who can diagram sentences with the smoothest facility, and spot the errors in the test sentences with never a miss, but whose own sentences are always clumsy, often illogical, and sometimes even ungrammatical. Analysis doesn't help much.

And exhortation doesn't help at all. No appeal to general principles, no mere pointing out and identifying of the phantoms, will exorcise them from a mind that has chosen, however unconsciously, to have them. We cannot get rid of them. They haunt our own minds. We must learn rather to live in lifelong struggle against them.

Happily, there are excellent weapons for the struggle, and a strategy that has always worked and still works when we try it. For not only is the style the man; the man is also the style, and we can clear our heads by clarifying our sentences. The thought is born with the sentence that constitutes it, or not at all: the sentence *is* the thought. Consciously and unconsciously, with various degrees of consciousness, we construct our thoughts: thinking is a process of composition. To a large extent, perceiving and even feeling are also processes of composition: intellectual processes. That is to say, they are matters of rule and convention. We can hardly make fine distinctions if we haven't mastered the agreement of subject and verb. We can express ourselves—create ourselves—only to the extent that we have mastered the rules and conventions of some language (or some other art, game or activity) well enough to play with them freely. Freedom is the ability to do what we want to do. We can achieve it only to the extent that we develop skill in doing something. The ability to express ourselves in writing comes gradually, as we master the language. The problem is not merely how to avoid errors but how to design structures: how to construct our thoughts: simple ones first, then increasingly complex and subtle ones. Not only analysis but also synthesis is what we need—and chiefly synthesis.

I have found that when students consciously try to work out certain traditional designs or structures they gradually learn how. In the process, they have to pay such close attention to form that they incidentally learn to avoid errors of grammar. It's impossible to write like Dr. Johnson if you make grammatical errors. In the process of learning to write like him, the students write grammatically as a matter of necessity, since the structure visibly sags or collapses wherever the grammar is weak. At first, to be sure, the sags and collapses are visible only to me; but they learn to see them when I point them out, and gradually, without my teaching them grammar, they learn to write grammatically. They retune their ears.

I give them examples of certain clearly marked styles; we analyze and imitate, doing what good writers have done: not in order to wind up writing like Dr. Johnson or Henry James or William Faulkner or Ernest Hemingway, but in order to discover some of the possibilities of English prose: to develop a consciousness of form and some skill in devising form, two things without which no individual style is possible. This is the method all good writers have used, instinctively or deliberately, in learning their common craft and developing their personal art.

We begin with some of the classic writers, whose symmetry, balance, parallelism and antithesis constitute to this day the basic form of Western thought: Isocrates, Cicero, Sallust, Seneca, Tacitus, Saint Ambrose, Saint Augustine, Saint Anselm of Canterbury, Bishop Latimer, Thomas Lever and Roger Ascham. (Observe how this chronological sequence leads the students from Greek and Latin into early English classicism.) Then we practice euphuism with Lyly, Greene, Lodge, Chettle and Florio, merely for the sake of the strenuous exercise. Then we practice some of the varieties of neo-classicism, with Newton, Dr. Johnson, Gibbon, Burke and Paine, and observe its continuing influence in such disparate nineteenth-century writers as Macaulay and P. T. Barnum. Then we try some varieties of poetic prose (the King James Bible, Lafcadio Hearn, Oscar Wilde, Francis W. Bain, Thomas Malory, James Joyce, Isak Dinesen, Vladimir Nabokov and Samuel Beckett); some Rabelaisian styles (Rabelais, Shakespeare, Dekker, Sterne, Melville and Joyce); some Victorian styles (Carlyle, Dickens, Ruskin and Henry James), and some twentieth-century styles (Joyce, Stein, Hemingway, Faulkner, Dos Passos, Beckett, Nabokov and Thorstein Veblen).

With such various materials, it is easy to find exercises for a wide variety of student predilections and special abilities; and the more deeply we go into any style the more predilections they discover. They are always delighted by the discovery of chiasmus, for example. The term *chiasmus,* derived from the Greek letter *chi* (X), signifies a crossing over or change of direction that not only avoids monotony but also sets up a pleasurable tension in the reader. By pointing out three examples widely separated in time—from Saint Augustine's *Confessions* (about A.D. 397), Joyce's *Ulysses* (1922) and Beckett's *How It Is* (French 1961, English 1964)—we give students a new respect for tradition and an unconscious desire to share in it. Here is Saint Augustine:

> In Thee abide, fixed for ever, the first causes of all things unabiding;
> and of all things changeable, the springs abide in Thee unchangeable:
> and in Thee live the eternal reasons of all things unreasoning and
> temporal.

Here we have two major crossings over or changes of direction, making two principal *chi*'s:

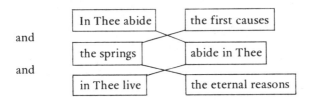

There is also, attached to one of these principal *chi*'s, a subordinate one:

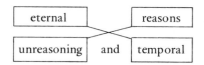

This is not just a fancy way of saying that only God is eternal and all nature merely a flickering emanation or shimmer of light from Him. It is Saint Augustine's personal way of saying it: an expression of his personality, in which at this far distant date we can still hear the reverent vibration of his voice. It is a late classic voice, perfectly conformed to the manner of the educated class in the late fourth century, but at the same time an individual voice, differing in clearly identifiable particular ways from that of his equally classical contemporary Saint Ambrose, for example. In teaching writing—or literature—it is vitally important to point out the individual differences as well as the generic similarities: the personal art as well as the common craft.

Students are deeply reassured and invigorated when they learn that two of the very best and most avant avant-garde twentieth-century writers use this traditional color of rhetoric. Here is Joyce:

> On Newcomen bridge the very reverend John Conmee S.J. of saint Francis Xavier's church, upper Gardiner street, stepped on to an outward bound tram.
> Off an inward bound tram stepped the reverend Nicholas Dudley C.C. of saint Agatha's church, north William street, on to Newcomen bridge.

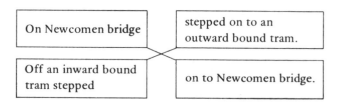

And here is Beckett. His nameless narrator hears, from within his head or without, he can't tell, a voice:

a voice which if I had a voice I might have taken for mine which at the instant I hear it I quote on is also heard by him whom Bom left to come towards me and by him to go towards whom Pim left me [.] [1]

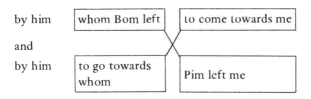

The antiquity of the rhetorical device notwithstanding, both these voices are unmistakably modern and each is unmistakably individual. The best modern writers write with great freedom because they have great discipline; most modern writers merely flounder, because they have none. That is largely the fault of us English teachers. Beginning on that ridiculous night when the sky was full of rhinestones and sequins, the night John Dewey was born, we stopped teaching the art of writing. Unlike the mathematicians, who are necessarily concerned with form, we let ourselves be seduced by big words like "ideas," "understanding," "self-expression" and "creativity," and we led students to believe that they could learn to write well without learning to write at all. College students are expected to learn calculus, but they are not expected to learn the artful uses of their native language. Perhaps half of our English majors have chosen English under the delusion that there isn't much to it; and to the extent that our unimaginative drudging laziness makes that delusion seem true we are betraying our students, ourselves, and all the humane values that inhere in our subject.

The remedy is in our own hands. The treatment I have described

1. From *How It Is* by Samuel Beckett, copyright © by Grove Press, Inc. Originally published under the title *Comment c'est,* copyright © by Les Editions de Minuit, Paris. Reprinted by permission of The Grove Press, Inc., and of Calder and Boyars, London.

is not a panacea; it will not cure those who are most deeply sunk in their neurotic servile need to be wrong, to speak and write like harmless plebeians or tame intellectuals; but our subconscious is not always beyond the reach of indirect influences; and I have found that a strenuous regimen of stylistic exercises does very noticeably help all but those whose minds are inert with caution.

# *The Avant-Garde*
## *as*
# *Conservators*

The great classic tradition of English prose is not dead. It is in living use. The antithetical style, which has been the basic form of Western thought since the afternoon of Athenian culture, is now being consciously cultivated—by a few avant garde writers. They practice it with an involuted fanciness that would have been considered decadent by the best Greek and Latin writers, but by contrast with the slack formlessness of our more conventional writers their conscious artfulness is a sign of vitality. The avant-garde alone is in touch with tradition. The avant-garde alone is preserving some continuity of development in English prose while more complacent writers are letting it fall into ruin. This is a usable fact of some importance for us who as English teachers struggle to make the next generation articulate.

We struggle too weakly; our aims are too modest. Most of our hard work is the automatic drudgery that is a form of laziness. Valery Larbaud's amusing billionaire A. O. Barnabooth, who notwithstanding his introspective ardors is accused by a popular journalist of living a life no different from that of "most of the idlers of his set," thinks briefly of replying, " 'Idle,' I who consume my

Reprinted by permission of The College English Association, Inc., © 1967.

life in pursuit of the absolute! It is you who are idle, poor hack bent
all night over a table." And we are idle in the same industrious way,
we who sit up half the night correcting the papers of students we
have been drilling in dullness half the day.

We are not wrong, we are necessarily right, to be concerned with
the placement of commas, the reference of relative pronouns, and
the agreement of subject and verb; but we are wrong in concentrat-
ing on a few such details to the exclusion of many others, and in
making too little of those few. We offer not too much but too little
formal grammar and rhetoric, and that little is often rejected because
in our exclusive devotion to it we make it seem irrelevant to
anything of consequence in our students' lives. We try to separate
form and content, which are integral and inseparable: we study
grammar as grammar, and literature as a source of wisdom or
morality or historical information or psychological insight, or worst
of all as a source of topics for themes.

But I have found that students master grammar easily enough if
we teach it not as a thing in itself but as a necessary element in a
more interesting task, and if accordingly we assume that they will
master it without our spending too much time on it. The more
interesting task is that of writing artfully: analyzing the art of
certain great writers and cultivating it—especially the antithetical art
that is the form of so much that is best in Western thought, and
most especially that of the brilliant classicists of our own day. Their
art, being alive and full of contemporary sense, is more accessible to
our students than the seemingly senseless rules of a grammar
seemingly unrelated to art or to anything else.

Our task is difficult because we approach it timidly. Many of our
students, the first in their families ever to go to college, are so
unfamiliar with standard college-graduate English that we must teach
it to them almost as if it were a foreign language. That is an
unavoidable difficulty, about which it is useless to complain and
unpardonable to sneer; but we often compound the difficulty by
adding to it another that is entirely factitious: we teach English as if
it were a dead language.

By a dead language I mean simply one that nobody speaks. Alas, I
don't mean one that nobody writes, for many people write

THE AVANT-GARDE AS CONSERVATORS

unspeakably, and many English teachers are among them. Many of us who speak normally enough write with the wooden stiffness of a seventeenth-century English schoolboy of ordinary ability writing correct Latin verse. The reason for this is that writing is not a natural activity like speech but an artificial activity that departs from speech. Writing English is easier than writing Latin, but just as artificial. Students who talk all the time and make themselves understood with no difficulty at all, but who don't write very much, have great difficulty making themselves understood in their native language when they have to write it. And many of us English teachers, whose profession requires us, if not to write, at least to correct the writing of students every day, write with no touch of nature, no sign of life, as if we had learned English out of a textbook. We punctuate not by ear but by rule, and the result is deadly; we construct our sentences with more regard to some non-writer's say-so than to our own breathing, and the result is prose that lacks the breath of life.

But of course we don't write with our lungs alone, we must also consult our brains; and when we apply our brains to the problem of getting the rhythms of life into our prose, we run into rules that cannot be ignored. We might as well try to play chess without rules. In order to write with some life, we must master the artificiality of the medium well enough to use it freely, to play with it, to spin curlicues and arabesques of variation on our themes: we must pass beyond the constraints of artificiality to the exuberance of artifice. This is largely a matter of practice: not the worse than futile practice that consists in repeating awkwardnesses over and over, but guided practice in constructing graceful structures.

I see that I must now define awkwardness and grace. Very well. There are two kinds of awkwardness: that of a person who forgets the beginning of the sentence before he reaches the end, and that of a person who applies a rule where it is not applicable. It is this second kind of awkwardness that many textbooks inculcate. Here are two examples from newspapers: (1) "The President and the Prime Minister conferred for two hours today and, over the weekend, they will confer more at length." (2) "Informed sources believe that the Governor will ask the legislature to increase taxes on all tobacco products or, at least, on cigarettes." The textbook rule our reporters have followed, which requires all such qualifying phrases as "over the weekend" and "at least" to be set off with commas, violates not only logic but also something much more basic to readable prose, the natural rhythm of human breathing. A comma indicates a pause; when we read these two sentences aloud we naturally pause in certain places; those places are where the commas belong: (1) "The President and the Prime Minister conferred for two hours today, and over the weekend they will confer more at length." (2) "Informed sources believe that the Governor will ask the Legislature to increase taxes on all tobacco products, or at least on cigarettes." And there is another reason for consulting our brains and our lungs instead of a rulebook in such matters: to pause after "and" in the first sentence, and "or" in the second, thus putting a meaningless emphasis on two mere conjunctions, is to have no sense of the uses of emphasis. No style, that is. No grace. No consciousness of what we are doing. False emphasis, false logic and false breathing will cause a few sensitive readers to reread and mentally repunctuate the sentences; many more readers, who are not aware of anything wrong, will nevertheless be jolted by the unnatural pauses, and in a relatively short time will be fatigued and stop reading. I have found that most of them call their fatigue boredom. Since they are interested in the subject matter, however, it is not boredom. It is fatigue, from a bumpy ride. Now we have our first definition. Awkward writing is writing that makes sensitive readers mentally rewrite and all readers lose interest.

And what is graceful writing? Well, we are two-sided animals, and Pascal observed some time ago that although we feel no need for a symmetry of top and bottom or front and back, we do feel a grateful pleasure, as at the gratification of a need, in symmetry that corresponds to our own—the symmetry of right and left. We are also—what with our breathing, our pulse, our walk, etc.—rhythmical animals, and we enjoy external rhythms and recurrences. Graceful writing is writing that gives us these two pleasures.

The good writers of the past were graceful; most writers of the present, having been miseducated, are not. But Samuel Beckett is. Alain Robbe-Grillet is. Michel Butor is. Günter Grass is. Heinrich

Böll is. John Hawkes is. Jorge Luis Borges is. A few others are. And they are all, as far as form goes, classicists. Their experiments are a resumption and a carrying forward of the living practices of the past. Here are a few illustrations from Beckett, who as the most consummate classicist of them all can stand for all.

1. His first published novel, *Murphy*, begins thus:

> The sun shone, having no alternative, on the nothing new. Murphy sat out of it, as though he were free, in a mew in West Brompton. Here for what might have been six months he had eaten, drunk, slept, and put his clothes on and off, in a medium-sized cage of north-western aspect commanding an unbroken view of medium-sized cages of south-eastern aspect. (Grove Press edition, p. 1.)

The antithesis in the last sentence, of "north-western" and "south-eastern," is fairly obvious. Less obvious but more delightful when we see them are the antitheses, in the first two, of "the sun" and "Murphy," "shone" and "sat out of it," and "having no alternative" and "as though he were free."

2. In his second published novel, *Watt*, he indicates Watt's tentative, hesitant habit by means of an excess of commas, and his unwearying explicitness by means of a pedantically balanced dialectic:

> Watt wore no tie, nor any collar. Had he had a collar, he would no doubt have found a tie, to go with it. And had he had a tie, he might perhaps have procured a collar, to carry it. But having neither tie, nor collar, he had neither collar, nor tie. (Grove Press edition, p. 219.)

3 and 4. Another classic device that Beckett uses is the periodic sentence. In *Murphy* and *Watt* the periods are complete, but in the later novels they begin to falter and fall to pieces. This one, from *Molloy*, falters: "That we thought of ourselves as members of a vast organization was doubtless also due to the all too human feeling that trouble shared, or is it sorrow, is trouble something, I forget the word." (Grove Press edition, p. 147.) [1] The faltering begins with the

---

1. From *Molloy* by Samuel Beckett, copyright © 1955 by Grove Press, Inc. Reprinted by permission of Grove Press, Inc. This acknowledgment applies to all other quotations from *Molloy* in this book.

repetition of sounds in "also due to the all too hu. . . ." And this one, from *The Unnamable,* starts out to be a magnificent structure, but Beckett deliberately smashes it: "The fact would seem to be, if in my situation one may speak of facts, not only that I shall have to speak of things of which I cannot speak, but also, which is even more interesting, but also that I, which is if possible even more interesting, that I shall have to, I forget, no matter." (Grove Press edition, p. 4.) [2]

Students respond to these inimitable brilliancies with such pleasure that it is then quite easy to lead them back to the imitable sources and start them writing in the classic mode. The common craft that underlies the individual styles of Isocrates, Cicero, St. Augustine and Dr. Johnson can be learned, as they learned it; the rhetoric of euphuism can be learned, as all too many learned it; the continuing influence of classicism can be discovered by analysis in such far and various offshoots as the Rabelaisian style of Renaissance bravado, the moralizing of Thoreau, the bombast of P.T. Barnum, the lyric prose of Lafcadio Hearn and the ironic solemnities of Thorstein Veblen, and all these and many others can be profitably imitated. The idea is not to wind up writing like Lyly or Dr. Johnson or Henry James, God forbid, but to understand and cultivate the tradition of symmetry from which all their diversities spring and in which they are united. I have tried this method, and it works. In becoming aware of the main tradition of English prose, and of some of its variations, students develop a sense of form and some facility in devising form. Thus they begin to have the technical resources with which to develop individual styles.

---

2. From *The Unnamable* by Samuel Beckett. Copyright © 1958 by Grove Press, Inc. Reprinted by permission of Grove Press, Inc. This acknowledgment applies to all other quotations from *The Unnamable* in this book.

# *Where Are All the Bossuets Gone?*

I wish the serious thinkers of our time would stop urging me to meet the challenge of the '70's. That is to say, I wish they wrote better. For there are a number of excellent magazines, full of information, inference and insight, such as *Daedalus* and *Foreign Affairs,* which I keep trying to read in order to strengthen my character and improve my mind and impress my friends, but I just can't. Their writers don't seem to enjoy writing. So I lay them wearily down and pick up something less formidable—less formidable because more formal, more felicitous, more humane, lighter, firmer, wittier—such as a funeral oration by Bossuet or a discussion of Platonic love by Plato.

Lightness is all, firmness is all, wit is all, exuberance is all; and these all inhere in strength of form. "That a man like me," says Beckett's Moran, "so meticulous and calm in the main, so patiently turned towards the outer world as towards the lesser evil, creature of his house, of his garden, of his few poor possessions, discharging faithfully and ably a revolting function, reining back his thoughts within the limits of the calculable so great is his horror of fancy, that a man so contrived, for I was a contrivance, should let himself be haunted and possessed by chimeras, this ought to have seemed strange to me and been a warning to me to have a care, in my own

interest. Nothing of the kind." (*Molloy*, Grove Press edition, p. 156.)
That sort of thing. It isn't funny, but it is witty, by virtue, the high
virtue, strength, efficacy, of its form. I wish our accredited thinkers
and spokesmen, our statesmen and their advisers, our scholars and
official prophets, had, if not Beckett's high virtue, at least some
stylistic sense. For how can they think without it? Certainly they
can't think to any humane purpose without it. The influence of
Hegel's thought has been altogether harmful, because his language is
suitable only for mystagogic bullfrogs and hippopotamuses bellow-
ing one mystique or another. But humane well-made language is not
beyond the means of normal human intelligence; all it takes—I am
not speaking of genius—is good training, good will, and careful
practice: for the avant-garde techniques of the very best contemporary writers are—after all—the traditional techniques of classicism. For syntax, there has never been a more purely classic writer
than Beckett. I turn to him for the same reason that I turn to
Bossuet. Good form carries everything with it, including that deep
conviction that cares nothing for mere facts. Such conviction comes
of joy. It is above facts, above evidence, above reason, above all
human sense and decency. What could be lighter, firmer, clearer,
cleaner, wittier, more exuberant and thus more compelling than
Bossuet's formal obsequies for the Duchess of Orleans? The verve
and restrained flourish of his control make every step of his proud
pavane an enchantment. If we weep, it is not for grief but for joy.
"Monseigneur," he begins, addressing the bereaved and yawning
Duke,

> I have been destined once again to perform this mournful duty, for the
> very high and very mighty Princess Henrietta Anna of England, Duchess
> of Orleans. She, whom I saw so attentive while I performed the same
> duty for the Queen her mother, was soon after to become the subject
> of a like discourse, and my sad voice was reserved to this deplorable
> ministry. O vanity! O nothingness! O mortals ignorant of their
> destinies! Would she have believed it ten months ago? And you,
> messieurs, would you have thought, when she was pouring out so many
> tears in this place, that she would reassemble you here to weep for her?
> Princess, worthy object of the admiration of two great kingdoms, was it
> not enough that England should weep for your absence without being
> constrained to weep still more for your death? And did not France,

which so joyfully received you surrounded with new splendor, welcome
with yet more pomps and triumphs your return from that famous
voyage from which you brought back so much glory and such great
hopes?

The famous voyage was to Dover in 1670, where she helped her
brother-in-law Louis XIV and her brother Charles II negotiate what
Winston Churchill was to call "the shameful treaty of Dover." But
no matter. Bossuet's oration is the rhetorical equivalent of Lebrun's
flattering frescoes at Versailles, and of Versailles itself, that supreme
achievement of solemn frippery. We need some solemn frippery
now. Our present conservatives aren't up to it. Listen briefly to
Richard Nixon's obsequies for Everett Dirksen: "Others will
remember the mastery of language, the gift of oratory that placed
him in a class with Bryan and Churchill, showing, as only he would
put it, that 'the oil can is mightier than the sword.' " This is more
shameful than the Treaty of Dover. We are perishing for lack of
style.

At this point, enchanted by my own solemn frippery, I read those
opening paragraphs to my wife—and she said, "I can see the readers
jumping all over you and saying, 'Write about the atom bomb that
way! Write about the ghettos with solemn frippery! Open the ivory
tower window, boy, and let the stench in!' " "You have just given
me my next paragraph," I said. "I'll quote you. Because you are
right, and we agree, and I was going to say something like that
anyhow. Only I was going to make a smooth, logical, natural,
persuasive transition. But your crude violence is more persuasive. It
makes a welcome, refreshing contrast. Thank you, ma'am."

Of course she is right. There are no contemporary Bossuets, and if
there were they neither could nor would say anything that might
help solve our problems or restore the health of our sick culture. But
the vitality of our language, which is essential to that of our culture,
is being maintained now by only a few writers, and at least half of
these are journalists and critics, whose work is necessarily subject to
loss of interest as the events and works they analyze recede from the
center of our attention. In any case, the vitality of language cannot
be merely maintained; from time to time it must be renewed and
re-created by great writers: a Chaucer, a Shakespeare, a Swift, a

Sterne, a Hawthorne, a Melville, a Conrad, a Joyce, a Faulkner. The only writers who are now renewing the vitality of English are Beckett and Nabokov; a dozen or so other writers of fiction are not sapping it; five or six poets are not sapping it; some twenty to thirty rightly distinguished journalists and critics are not sapping it; a few scholars are not sapping it; everybody else who writes is in one way or another sapping it.

Once, at another university than the one at which I now teach, I rejected on behalf of the graduate school's literacy committee a Ph.D. dissertation that had been accepted by the sociology department; it contained many vile phrases, one of which I still too vividly remember: "It was decided to make this criteria non-criterial." I have never seen anything quite that bad in any published book of non-fiction, even of sociology; but many of us academics write our native language with little more feeling than the author of that deservedly Unpubl. Diss. Consider: a well-known professor of education (Patricia Sexton) at a major university (N.Y. Univ.), in a serious book (*The Feminized Male*) published by a major publisher (Random House), repeatedly uses "lay" for "lie," repeatedly refers to the range of boys' and girls' interests as "the masculinity-femininity continuum," and repeatedly calls her questionnaires "scales," as in this quite typical sentence: "A masculinity-femininity scale was also given to all ninth-grade students." [1]

And what harm does a little scientific-sounding pretentiousness do? Though the vocabulary is inaccurate and the syntax stiff, this prose is not unintelligible. The author knew what she meant, the publisher's editor knew what she meant, we all know what she meant. The communication would seem to be pragmatically perfect. But it isn't. It overlookd the fact that at least some readers have active minds, not mere passive tape recorders or oscillographs between their ears. Communication through speech or writing is always complex: there are always at least two messages: and in this case the secondary message undercuts the author's authority by telling us that she is a creator of jargon, a person who has an instinct for jargon as the accident-prone have an instinct for falling down

---

1. From *The Feminized Male* by Patricia Sexton. Copyright © 1969 by Patricia Sexton. Reprinted by permission of Patricia Sexton and of Random House, Inc.

stairs, a graceless pedant, a clumsy barbarian, an enemy alike of masculinity and femininity, intellect and healthy instinct, sophistication and innocence, art and nature.

To whom does her prose tell all these things? "Us," I said. And just who the hell, pray tell, are we? Well, obviously, we are the readers who see that her vocabulary is inaccurate and her syntax stiff and are not favorably impressed by that low mannerism the impersonal passive. Evidently there aren't many of us; and if the majority, which determines usage, is indifferent, by what right do we say that its indifference is unfortunate because some usages are wrong? Many graduate students of English now say "analyzation" instead of "analysis," and some torture themselves, the English language and me with clumsy inventions such as "parodize," "parodization," "caricaturize" and "caricaturization." I know perfectly well what they mean when they utter such sounds, and if their usages should become predominant wouldn't my continuing protests against their unconscious affectation be the merest nit-picking pedantry?

No. Usage be damned. As a simple objective matter of fact, such humbug words are objectively wrong. A word is not always or merely an arbitrary thing, a matter of convention and nothing more; it is a product not only of history and custom but also of reason and design and sometimes even of nature; we need only consult an etymological dictionary to see that such well-designed synthetic words as "analysis," "parody" and "caricature" are what they are because that is what they should be. To add syllables to them, whether through ignorance or ostentation or both, is to damage for no good purpose good and useful products of human ingenuity; if the damage is not apparent to those who do it, or to their naive readers, it is nevertheless apparent to skillful writers and precise readers, who value the English language's well-made words and fine distinctions because they lend themselves to precision of thought and subtlety of expression, two necessities of independent life. Of course we can't require everybody to take a course in English philology and be conscious of the rationale of every word and write accordingly; forbidding the distortion of words by ignorant analogy or irresponsible pomposity is as vain as forbidding the tide to rise; but a distortion does in fact damage the instrument we must all use.

Of course there are complications. I spoke, for example, of Bossuet's "obsequies" for the Duchess of Orleans, knowing full well that—strictly speaking—the right word would be "exequies"; but "obsequies," though its use here is objectively wrong, and though such use has indeed robbed the English language of a distinction as valid as the all but lost distinctions between "disinterested" and "uninterested" and "flaunt" and "flout," has now so entirely replaced "exequies" that to use the right word would be more pedantic than useful. I have therefore surrendered the dead "exequies," though I still stubbornly keep in my vocabulary the not quite dead "uninterested" and "flout." We must always be aware of what we are doing and why.

But increasing numbers of writers don't know what they are doing. The distortion of words is only one of many symptoms of a widespread and spreading slackness, carelessness, indifference and incompetence with language. In Bossuet's day the generality of ordinary writers maintained—by their mere practice, custom and example—a kind of minimum standard of skill. Few of them could dance with anything like Bossuet's grace, but all of them could walk without staggering, lurching, stumbling or falling down. They were not great swordsmen, but they could walk sideways through a narrow doorway without getting their swords tangled between their legs. That is more than can be said of most writers now writing in English; and their bad examples are so suggestive, if only because of their number, that they have even affected the practice of their betters—including writers whose very subject is precision of thought. One of the best of these is Richard Robinson. His *Definition* (Oxford, 1954) is a book I like, admire, and use; it has helped me a great deal, and I highly recommend it to anyone who cares for precision in his own thinking; but even it has sloppinesses here and there. Here are four examples from the chapter on stipulative definitions:

(1) Since then stipulation has bad effects as well as good, and is therefore not entirely free, can we give ourselves rules to follow in order to secure more of its good and less of its bad results? [P. 80.] [2]

2. All quotations from *Definition* by Richard Robinson. Reprinted by permission of The Oxford University Press, London.

Here the phrase "since then" doesn't have its usual temporal sense, but we naturally read it in that sense; and though we then immediately see our mistake and re-read, mentally supplying a pair of commas and getting the pedantic form "Since, then, stipulation . . . ," we have nevertheless been delayed, however briefly; we have nevertheless had to do the author's work for him, though the strain was not great; and we have wound up with a pedantry, though an amusing one. Here we have a minor clumsiness, which could have been avoided in any one of a number of ways—such as "Stipulation thus has bad effects as well as good; can we give ourselves rules. . . ?" (Incidentally, he doesn't mean "less"; he means "fewer.")

> (2) After such a redefinition of "empirical" or "selfish" or "certain," it is still necessary to use the word occasionally in the old sense, because the old sense indicated a distinction that really existed and was very important to us. [Pp. 83—4.]

Here too we mentally rewrite, changing "it is still necessary to use the word occasionally" to "it is still occasionally necessary to use the word," in order to avoid any possibility, however slight and unlikely, that some reader somewhere at some time under some circumstances might just conceivably read "It is still necessary to use the word 'occasionally.' " Read the sentence aloud and you'll see that the possibility exists. In good writing it shouldn't.

> (3) Professor Dubs writes that "editors and reviewers should police philosophical writings; any article failing to define its terms clearly or unnecessarily departing from established meanings of words should be considered unworthy of being offered to the public." [P. 87.]

Here we correct Professor Dubs' unintended phrase "failing to define its terms unnecessarily" by mentally rewriting: "failing to define its terms clearly or departing unnecessarily." We also observe with despair that Professor Robinson has put the "that" of indirection before a direct quotation—and him a logician and all.

> (4) When we need a name for something which has previously not had a name, is it better to invent a new word or to use an old word in the new sense? Is it better, for example, to call a new weapon of war a

"bazooka" (assuming this to be a new sound) or to call it a "tank," using an old word in a new sense? [P. 87.]

Here the syntax implies that there is only one new weapon ("it") and that the army nomenclature specialists are wondering whether to call it a bazooka or a tank. We don't mentally rewrite this one, because the process would be too complicated; we just say to ourselves, "He means there are two weapons, not one." He could have obviated our momentary confusion by writing something like this: "In naming new weapons, for example, the army sometimes invents a new word, as in the case of 'bazooka' (which I assume was a new sound); sometimes it uses an old word in a new sense, as in the case of 'tank.' Which method is better?" Put thus clearly, the illustration is obviously a poor one, since in these particular cases both methods are quite satisfactory; but at least the syntax doesn't change the intended substance. Here we see how bad syntax sometimes fails to prevent our choosing bad material.

Professor Robinson is by no means the only contemporary scholar concerned with precision of language who sometimes uses it imprecisely. The deliberately belletristic C. S. Lewis, who when he writes about literature is always intelligent and usually humane, is at his best in *An Experiment in Criticism*. The intolerance that chills his religious books and his novels appears here only as an amusing smugness. In these pages he is often smug but seldom clumsy. But in our age the prevalent carelessness is such that even he, on page 99 for example, is unintentionally funny: "The ancient city states developed, under the spur of practical necessity, great skill in speaking so as to be audible and persuasive to large assemblies in the open air." [3] The confusion here is due to an unconscious personification, and behind the personification is the assumption of scholastic realism that a city state is a thing in itself, not a collection of individuals; it is a striking example of the frequent reciprocity of metaphorical fantasy and imprecise language; but regardless of philosophy, the sentence as it stands is nonsensical. On the next page

3. Both quotations from C. S. Lewis: *An Experiment in Criticism*, © 1961, 1965, Cambridge University Press. Reprinted by permission.

Lewis says that some lovers of poetry ask, "Why should I turn from a real and present experience—what the poem means to me, what happens to me when I read it—to inquiries about the poet's intention or reconstructions, always uncertain, of what it may have meant to his contemporaries?" Having been misled into reading "inquiries about the poet's reconstructions," we re-read and do our own reconstructing: we insert "to" before "reconstructions" and proceed somewhat displeased, our pleasure having been interrupted by a moment of annoyance at a good writer who has made an elementary mistake and allowed it to go through. But we do take pleasure in *An Experiment in Criticism,* and pleasure of an austerer kind in *Definition;* their occasional infelicities are all due to the epidemic clumsiness that infects our age through the contagion of example, rather than to the congenital clumsiness of the non-verbal.

How much pleasanter our life would be if the non-verbal didn't insist on writing! But they do: some write textbooks of English composition, and others, no better, write novels. It is in the nature of English for many nouns, such as "telephone" and "radio," to be used as verbs; but others, such as "automobile" and "airplane," are not naturally so used; "cart," yes; "car," no; "box," yes; "basket," no; "crate," yes; "trunk," no; people who have normal natures and a normal facility with their native language know instinctively which nouns will do and which will not do as verbs, just as continental Europeans, we are told, know instinctively the gender of a noun they see or hear for the first time; but many people with no nature in them, whose facility with their native language is unmistakably subnormal—writers of position papers, for example—have imposed their subnormal ways on so much of our public utterance that our linguistic nature is in danger of being perverted. Three or four years ago my son closed a copy of *Time* and said, "People who use 'structure' as a verb are innately depraved." Every day since then has brought forth more evidence that he was right. Listen to this depraved utterance from a current textbook of English composition, H. Ross Winterowd's *Structure, Language, and Style:*

> Dictionaries, then, seldom help us with the sum total of meaning
> when one word is structured with another word or when five words are

structured with five other words or when ten words are structured with
ten more words. . . . Words meet, merge, and transcend themselves.[4]

The dots don't indicate a hiatus or an ellipsis: they are Winterowd's
own. I don't know what his last sentence here means, but I suspect
it's something dirty.

His book, however, is at least as good as nine out of ten others in
its field. If we get such pitiful slop from teachers of English, what
can we expect of mere novelists, poets and playwrights? The
incoherence of much that passes for poetry now is well known;
every good theater critic has observed the illiteracy of many current
and recent plays; and here are a few of many passages that might be
adduced from current and recent novels:

> Beside me at the rail, brown hands accepted the holy wafer. . . .
> Then, momentarily, it lay at my own palm's heart. . . . A white woman
> with two blond-haired girls sat in the second row. The woman was
> kneeling. [D. Keith Mano, *Horn,* p. 76.] [5]

> My kneecaps danced, slapping together in my lap. [*Horn,* p. 216.]

> He lay on his back, starry-eyed. "Ah," he said, from his prone
> position. [Pamela Hansford Johnson, *The Survival of the Fittest,* p. 48.
> Even if we overlook the corn, are we to lie supinely down and accept
> the obliteration of a useful distinction without protest?] [6]

> Her hair, glossy, low curled now in her nape, tossed away the
> lamplight. [*The Survival of the Fittest,* p. 121.]

> A train arrives, a passenger departs and is met by a real-estate agent
> named Hazzard. [John Cheever, *Bullet Park,* p. 4. He means a passenger
> gets off; if he wants to be formal, why doesn't he say "descends"?
> Anything but "departs."] [7]

4. From Winterowd, H. Ross, *Structure, Language and Style, A Rhetoric-Handbook,* 1969, Dubuque, Iowa, Wm. C. Brown Company Publishers. Reprinted by permission.

5. Both quotations from *Horn* by D. Keith Mano. Copyright © 1969 by Houghton Mifflin Co. Reprinted by permission of Houghton Mifflin Co.

6. Both quotations from *The Survival of the Fittest* by Pamela Hansford Johnson. Reprinted by permission of Charles Scribner's Sons, New York, and of Macmillan, London and Basingstoke, England.

7. All quotations from *Bullet Park* by John Cheever. Copyright © 1969 by Alfred A. Knopf, Inc. Reprinted by permission of Alfred A. Knopf, Inc.

He gets out of bed for the third time, returns to the kitchen and makes some coffee. He brings a cup for them both. [*Bullet Park,* p. 9. These are well-to-do people; surely they can afford two cups. And surely Cheever was capable of writing "He brings a cup for each of them." Apparently he just didn't care.]

His male member . . . was a domesticated organ with a love of home cooking, open fires and the thighs of Nellie. [*Bullet Park,* p. 24. Let's hope he doesn't dip it in the boeuf bourguignon or roast it too long at the open fire. There may be an allusion in those thighs to the Earl of Rochester, but that doesn't excuse such innocence.]

The effect was like stretching an already tensioned spring. [Arthur Hailey, *Airport,* Bantam edition, p. 83. Stop tensioning that spring, you fool!] [8]

Traffic, he observed, was averagely busy for the time of day. [*Airport,* p. 147. He means it was about as busy as usual, or no busier than usual, for the time of day. But traffic is neither busy nor idle, but light or heavy. Perhaps he should say "Traffic, he observed, was about average for the time of day."]

As the door slammed closed, . . . [*Airport,* p. 211. This isn't unintelligible or misleading; it merely illustrates the fatal need of the non-verbal to avoid the precise word: there is no possibility whatever that a writer like Hailey could say, "The door slammed shut."]

Etc., etc. There are, to be sure, hopeful signs. *The Survival of the Fittest,* though marred here and there by blunders such as those I have cited, is a much smoother performance than any of Miss Johnson's previous novels, in which there are two, three or four blunders per page, or than any of the other novels from which I have just quoted; and anybody who enjoys good language can read with pleasure such novels as Jeff Nuttall's *Pig,* Tom Raworth's *A Serial Biography,* John Hawkes' *The Lime Twig,* Evan S. Connell, Jr.'s *Mr. Bridge,* and Peter Najarian's *Voyages;* but such consistently good performances are rare in current fiction, and from day to day they constitute smaller and smaller fractions of the larger and larger stacks of novels the publishers shove at us.

---

8. All quotations from *Airport* by Arthur Hailey. Copyright © 1968 by Arthur Hailey, Ltd. Reprinted by permission of Doubleday & Co., Inc.

But the chief threat to the quality of our language, and hence of our thought, our feeling, our life, inheres not in the infelicities of novelists, poets and playwrights, whom most of us read only on weekends or at odd hours if at all, but in the meaningless resonances of serious thinkers to whom we give our serious attention every day: such intellectual leaders as (1) Richard Nixon again, who said in awarding a Presidential Unit Citation to the First Regiment of the First Marine Division, "I trust that the political leadership that we have in this country will be able to match the sacrifice that they have made"; (2) Bob Odell, football coach of the University of Pennsylvania, who said in announcing that a star player would either have to get a haircut or leave the team, "I told him that I felt appearance, dedication and sacrifice were also important parts of the program"; (3) Barry Goldwater, a Senator of the United States, who said of the Paris peace talks, "It is high time we told the people in Paris to fish or cut bait"; and (4) Robert M. Hutchins, who keeps urging me to subscribe to the magazine of the Center for the Study of Democratic Institutions so I can read "a continuing dialogue"—at this point I dropped his solicitation into the waste basket; later I went out to the garage and dug it out of the trash can, thinking it might provide an illustration for this piece, which I was then beginning to compose—and boy, does it!—"a continuing dialogue in which are examined the major institutions of the 20th Century in the light of their impact on democracy. Here are risen [sic] the great questions of the day—war and peace, church and state, automation and human values, race and revolution. As you can imagine, these discussions are lively, the observations and conclusions arresting and thought-provoking."

I'd rather not imagine, if you don't mind; I'd rather lie down and close my eyes so I won't see anything in the light of an impact, and hope I won't hear any great questions being risen. I wish Nixon, Odell, Goldwater, Hutchins and all the other serious thinkers of our time would stop challenging me, stop trying to provoke me to thought with their lively discussions and arresting conclusions, and go away with their continuing dialogue. I long to hear it fading away in the distance.

As far as language goes, I prefer the plain stupidity and ugly

Eichmann-like lowness of the Green Beret Captain Budge E. Williams, who said after the murder charge was dropped, "I regard all my enemies as dangerous. When you find one, you kill him. That's what they pay me for, not to worry about his social problems"—and the Bruno-Mussolini-like sexual tastes of Colonel George S. Patton III, who has said in Vietnam that he doesn't hate the enemy, "but I do like to see the arms and legs fly." What would he like to see if he hated them?

The Williamses and Pattons are always with us, but we don't always respect them. They don't always find it politic to expose themselves so shamelessly. The fact that they now do indicates a desperate sickness in our culture, which will not be cured by the wisdom of all our Nixons, Goldwaters, Odells and Hutchinses. I see more honor, more strength, more grace, more wit, more humane intelligence, more hope for the future of our species, in the inarticulate obscenities of our fed-up youth. We must give them language. Thus far we have not. That's why they don't see the reactionary implications of their revolutionary aims.

# *Social Class in the English Class*

We English teachers have always been subject to populist scorn and suspicion, and today the difficulty of our work is compounded by the populists' growing confidence that they are right and by our growing realization that they are not altogether wrong. And nevertheless, with regard to the uses of language, they *are,* basically, fundamentally, in principle and in most applications, wrong. The more their confidence grows, the wronger they are—and the more complicated the problem of teaching their naive followers becomes. What must we do to counteract the old populist scorn of verbal precision now that it is supported by a resumption of the reactionary nineteenth-century campaign to derange our senses and hallucinate our perceptions? How must we treat the old servile need to be intellectually harmless now that it is complicated once again by the recurrent mystical need to be mentally drunk? How can we help students develop an ear for good language, a respect for the skill of good writers, a desire to write skillfully themselves, now that their vocabulary is atrophied, their syntax crippled, and their prosody non-existent?

In Marguerite Duras' novel *Moderato Cantabile* a piano teacher shows a little boy how to play a passage but he refuses even to put his hands on the keyboard. "You'll never learn to play the piano if you don't try," says the teacher. "I don't want to learn to play the piano," says the boy; and the situation is such that we sympathize equally with both. As English teachers we are up against a psychological problem analogous to that of the piano teacher. We need to develop sympathy, tact, and that inner authority which no outer authority can replace. We must also polish up our neglected arrogance. In many cases the populists' arguments deserve serious consideration and action; in other cases neither their arguments nor their motives deserve anything but contempt—an attitude which, since we are painfully unaccustomed to it, we must willfully cultivate. "Sir," said Dr. Johnson, "treating your adversary with respect is giving him an advantage to which he is not entitled." Thus he made clear a disadvantage we devotees of language and literature suffer in arguing with disingenuous enemies of language and literature, who fear nothing so much as the disinterested sensitivity to intellectual quality we try to develop in our students. We must throw off this unfair disadvantage. We must stop trying to accommodate our discipline to the unaccommodating; we must stop trying to come to a reasonable understanding with the unreasonable; we must stop trying to come to terms with the interminable. For in our arguments with them we too enjoy an unfair advantage: we are right. Moreover, our poor innocent mixed-up students are not our intellectual equals; we must no longer listen to them as if they were, and we must try to strengthen the spines of our colleagues who do.

All inner authority flows from sympathy. We must be aware of the strong points in our adversaries' position; we must state their arguments more clearly and forcefully than they themselves are able to state them; this is easy enough to do, and the very doing of it demonstrates the superior strength of our own position: a position worked out with full awareness of what is valid in linguistic populism and what is not. Such awareness makes the difference between authority and authoritarianism.

One of our neighbors recently called out to another, who was sitting in a lawn chair behind a hedge, "Who are you hiding from?" Is there anybody in the English-speaking world who really thinks he should have said, "From whom are you hiding?" If so, I hope that unfortunate person is not an English teacher. One Sunday afternoon while our car was being gassed up I walked into the filling station and asked—well, I started to ask, "Have you any flashlight batteries?" But then I thought I'd better speak the language of the people to whom I was speaking, I mean like talk the language of the guys I was talking to, so I asked, "Have you got any flashlight batteries?"

If I had any skill with the techniques of avant-garde fiction I could convey the simultaneity of all this, but fiction requires as special a talent as poetry—think of the brilliant expository prose and the cardboard fiction of C. P. Snow, Mary McCarthy, Edmund Wilson, James Baldwin, George Orwell and John Hersey—so here goes with the plain old brilliant expository prose. While waiting for the batteries I thought of a story of Valery Larbaud, who enjoyed speaking the language of whatever country he was in, with an accent, idiom and intonation appropriate to his interlocutor. Once a Belgian train conductor said to him, "You speak French very well, for a Frenchman. I mean, you speak it without an accent—like us. You don't Frentify it—*vous ne le frantisez pas.*" I was trying to follow Larbaud's example, but I didn't quite make it. For my inter-locutor. . . . You see what I mean? "Interlocutor," he says. With a vocabulary like that there, how the hell can you talk natural? . . . Now where was I? I mean, like where the fuck was I at? . . . Why was I trying to talk like the filling station man, anyhow? My idiom is as natural to me as his is to him, and in my vain effort to talk like him I was putting on airs. . . . So my interlocutor turned to his partner and said, "Whur's the flashlight battries at?" That's wonderful, I thought in my pedantic way: a sentence of five and a half words, with two mispronunciations and two grammatical errors; but his partner immediately topped it by pointing to a box and uttering a sentence of two and a half words with three grammatical errors: "Them's them."

Grammatical errors? The communication was perfect. I got the batteries. What more is speech supposed to do? What more can it do than convey information perfectly? Ah, but it also conveys another kind of information: it tells us who the speaker is. That is *the* unmentionable fact in our freshman English classes. The man who said "Them's them" has been communicating whatever he wanted to communicate all his life with no difficulty whatever, and now his son is in college and has blackened the wrong spaces on the placement-test answer sheet so we tell him his English won't do and we put him in a no-credit remedial English course. By so doing, we create what our journalists call a credibility gap. His English has always done. Why the hell won't it do? His gentle girl-graduate instructor would never dream of telling him. Perhaps she herself has never had the courage to know. So she says, "Well, if you write incorrectly you won't be able to do college work: you won't pass your other courses." That is theoretically true. But at their next interview he shows her a history bluebook full of grammatical errors, misspellings, incoherencies, statements that say the opposite of what he obviously meant to say, and inaccuracies of vocabulary that make many of his grammatical statements meaningless—and it bears the grade B. The awarding of that grade was of course a crime against the university and against society, if not against the student himself, but I suppose we all know by now that it does no good to urge our colleagues in other departments to insist on good English. What is good English, anyhow? With all his bad English, the student did in fact indicate to the history teacher's satisfaction that his information was 80 percent correct; and was the teacher to grade him less than 80 percent because he said, "The colonys had to fight for independent when the parlment encroched the rights weather the wanted to or not"? Or even, "The sothern colonys would not fight the yanky officers ordring the men around so it was lucky it was Geo Washington comander in cheif then the fought because he was the best one it was politics"? If the history teacher, remembering his own lecture, can figure out what the student intended to say, and if the information seems to him not wrong—i.e., if he believes that the student was trying to say that the choice of George Washington as commander-in-chief was a political choice intended to secure the adherence of the Southern colonies, but that it was nevertheless a fortunate choice because he was probably the best man for the job—then should the teacher refuse to admit that the student has this information? Or that—though he hasn't stated it clearly—he seems to have it about right, say at a guess 80 percent right? Let me say at once, lest there be any misapprehension, that at Temple University and I should think at most other universities no student who continues to write like that can get through, because unless he learns to write with reasonable clarity he will never get out of English R and never be allowed to take English 1, which does after all assume a higher level of accomplishment. Few cases are so bad, anyhow. But many are almost that bad, and it does no good to ask our colleagues in other departments to make common cause with us for decent standards of written and spoken English. We can and do argue that a student whose language is muddled cannot have a very clear understanding of anything that has to be put into words. We can and do refer to Peirce's statement, "It is wrong to say that . . . good language is *important* to good thought, merely; for it is of the essence of it." We can and do point out that if a student writing an undergraduate English term paper on Milton should get his historical facts wrong it would lower his grade, no matter how sensitive to Milton's language he might be. All our arguments are useless. Our colleagues in other departments do in fact make not only a valid distinction between information and the language in which it is conveyed, but also a quite invalid distinction between thought and the language that constitutes it. So that we must undertake alone the hard job of clarifying our students' language and the thought it constitutes.

There are two reasons for using the so-called "correct" forms of English, one good and one bad. Our students are vaguely aware of the bad one and totally unaware of the good one. We must overcome our reluctance and face whatever danger there may be and show them that we too are aware of the bad one and that we scorn it as much as any of them and more than some of them. Then we must show them the good one and convince them of its value.

The bad one is of course the snob appeal of the so-called "correct" forms. Why should the filling station man not have said "Them's them"? What should he have said? "Those are they"? "There they are"? "Them's them" is better, not only for its effectiveness as what Thorstein Veblen calls "direct and forcible speech," but even for its integrity of form. Its purely literary value, in terms of euphony, concision, balance and emphasis, is much higher than that of either of the two alternatives I have mentioned. But its social value is very low indeed. To say "Them's them," except as a joke, is a social error. It is lower class. I shall not go into the reasons, which have been clearly set forth by Veblen in *The Theory of the Leisure Class* (Modern Library edition, n.d., pp. 45–46, 398–400), by J. Vendryes in *Language* (Barnes & Noble edition, 1951, pp. 239–44), by Richard Robinson in *Definition* (Oxford, 1954, pp. 37–38, 56), and by Nancy Mitford in *Noblesse Oblige* (Harper, 1956, passim), among others. Suffice it here to recall the fact that from the social point of view one usage is "correct" and another "incorrect" for the same reason that one way of holding a fork is "correct" and another "incorrect": the "correct" way is the way of the upper and upper middle classes. Our universities have traditionally assumed and taught the English of those classes; many of our students now resent this fact, and I for one will not say they are wrong. Some of the best, kindest, most intelligent and most effective people I know—good friends, good neighbors, good spouses, good parents, good citizens, and economically quite well off, thank you—don't speak "correct" English, have never read a line of Shakespeare, and have never heard of Plato. On the other hand, we all know some real drips whose speech and writing, though neither vigorous nor beautiful, are absolutely "correct," and who exclude "incorrect" speakers and writers from all human consideration. It behooves us to remember that T. S. Eliot's world ended with a sneer. Our profession is damaged by teachers who share none of Eliot's talents except the one for sneering. With whatever small degree of justice, large numbers of students now associate our insistence on the "correct" forms with social snobbery. This is a fact we must all be increasingly aware of; the problems it creates should be matters of the most serious, urgent concern to the National Council of Teachers of English, the College English Association, the Modern Language Association, the International Association of University Professors of English, and other professional bodies—matters not for years or decades of leisurely research—whose data will be out of date by the time they are published, so that more research will be necessary because of course we wouldn't want to act on the basis of out-of-date data—but for immediate, practical, effective action: for if we don't soon solve the problems, or soon help the students solve them, they will soon solve them in their own way—and we won't like the solutions.

We won't like them because the students in their disaffection with all proprieties of language will destroy the valid along with the silly, the useful along with the useless, the good along with the bad. Therefore, we cannot afford the indulgence of phony corporate solutions couched in what Walker Gibson calls "committee neutralese" and adorned with graphs to make them still less readable: we must present our own good simple reasons for maintaining what is left of the traditional clarity, beauty, precision and force of the English language and regaining as much as possible of what has recently been lost.

Above the level of remedial English, most of our students' mistakes are not lapses of grammar or of linguistic decorum but inaccuracies of vocabulary. At a recent meeting of my graduate seminar in contemporary experimental writers, a student spoke of Robbe-Grillet's "cosmology." When I asked what he meant, since Robbe-Grillet isn't concerned with cosmology, he said, "You know—his world view." When I pointed out that the vague term "world view," whatever it may mean, certainly doesn't mean cosmology, which has to do with the nature of the cosmos or universe, the position of the earth in space, the motion of the planets, etc., he shrugged and continued as if I had made a vain distinction where there was really no difference. Perhaps he thought, "As long as you know what I mean, what difference does it make whether I say 'cosmology' or 'world view'?" But I hadn't known what he meant. I had been baffled by a misleading word, just as I would have been baffled if he had tried to indicate a chair by the word "table." I was embarrassed to make such an elementary distinction, but he wasn't embarrassed at all. I assumed that the other students also had been baffled by the sentence, but since the whole issue was a digression I didn't belabor it; afterwards, however, it occurred to me that perhaps two or three of them had not been baffled: that having been long habituated to cloudy imprecision, in which words mean whatever we vaguely want them to mean, they had vaguely inferred from the context the general drift, and the general drift had been enough. I know that that was not the case with most of the students, but even in graduate classes now there are some who I fear have become incapable of distinguishing one idea from another: i.e., of clearly understanding any idea, or even of feeling a need to understand it clearly. And I am afraid this relaxed habit of mind is spreading. The first time a graduate student told me he took Madame Blavatsky's *Isis Unveiled* seriously, I laughed and didn't believe it; but now we know only too well that theosophy is as popular as astrology and the Tarot cards. My chief objection to such sideshow stuff is that it blows their vocabularies. Logicians from Aristotle onward have been concerned over the effects on our thought of nouns for which there are no corresponding objects—not only of names for abstractions, such as *animal, tool* and *liquid,* and for nonentities, such as *gallon, mile* and *hour,* but even more of names for mythical beings, such as *chimaera, sphinx, unicorn, leprechaun, kobold, mermaid, siren* and *virgin.* By using such nouns, we fill our private world with non-existent objects: we create for ourselves delusions and even on occasion hallucinations. As Dostoievsky says somewhere, the question is not whether we believe that ghosts are seen, but whether we believe that they exist. How can a person perceive the world clearly, or—which is even more important—write clearly, if his head is full of karma and dharma and he therefore believes that the world is full of them too? The elementary logical distinction between words and things, which students often forget in the haste or heat or agony or indifference of composition, disappears entirely when they blow their minds—i.e., their vocabularies—with such paltry stuff. The ways of genius are of course unaccountable: a Blake or a Yeats, having absolute and as it were instinctive command of language, can create beauty from nothing more than his own delusions; but a person whose command of language is shaky—who says, for example, and I quote, that a man of integrity is "integrious" and that meat-eating is "dilatorious" to the health—would do better to stay within the generous limits of the observable and the demonstrable.

To the extent that we think in words, language is an instrument of perception as well as of expression. A thought we can't express is one we don't quite understand, not having worked it out. Working it out involves constructing it as a sentence or a series of sentences. If we lack the appropriate words, and have little skill in the syntactic arrangement of such words as we have, not only can we not express nuances of thought and feeling, we can't even experience them. To the extent that we think in words, the quality of our thought inheres in that of our language; and all truths above the level of proverbs (which as Coleridge observed are frequently not true anyhow) are of the nature of nuances. The English language, having absorbed words, roots, prefixes, infixes and suffixes from many others, is rich, not poor; but in order to enjoy its riches we must command them. To be able to say "glad," "happy," "gay" and "joyful," "fortunate," "lucky," "happy" and "felicitous," "wish," "want," "desire" and "crave," "watch," "look at," "observe," "contemplate" and "regard," "under," "underneath," "beneath" and "below," "over," "above," "atop" and "on top of," "incomplete," "uncompleted" and "unfinished," "kin," "relatives" and "family," "number," "quantity" and "amount," "deadly," "mortal" and "fatal," "spell," "hex" and "enchantment," "kingly," "royal" and "regal," "vow" and "swear," "vow" and "oath," "right" and "just," "freedom" and "liberty," "sleeping" and "dormant," "drowsing" and "dozing," "impossible" and "not possible," "dangerous" and "hazardous," "risky" and "chancy," "less" and "fewer," "partly" and "partially," "fully," "completely," "wholly," "entirely," "altogether" and "absolutely"—to be able to choose from two or more combinations of connotations, rhythms and tone colors, as well as among niceties of denotation—makes writing and speaking well a joy. Needless to say, we are not born with a desire for this particular joy. It must be cultivated and acquired. Helping our students cultivate and acquire it is difficult at best; we must not make it more difficult by hobbling each other with prescriptions and proscriptions. Since enthusiasm on our part is absolutely essential, each of us must be free to teach in his or her own way, and we must respect our individual differences. My own predilection being what it is, to most of my students the joy of playing with sentence patterns seems to come more easily than that of distinguishing between "perhaps" and "maybe"; but my colleague Howard Meroney, in his graduate seminar in English philology, has his students try to establish doubtful etymologies; they work with a wide range of lexicons and etymological dictionaries, starting with what they call "kid stuff like Skeat" and proceeding to Holthausen, Kluge, Walde and others; and in their conversation out of class they refer to these exercises so often, and always with such enthusiasm, that it is quite evident that they suffer joy. Part of their joy is also quite evidently due to their admiration of Meroney, and I am not suggesting that any number of etymological dictionaries can take the place of an excellent teacher. But I myself still remember the thrill—the rush of blood to the face, the tingling in the scalp—I experienced on first looking into Skeat. "This," I thought, "is something like reading *Finnegans Wake!*" And my friend Dr. George Cannon, whose interests have to do with medicine, education and the race problem rather than with philology, once told me that he still remembers with pleasure, every time he passes a stone wall, a high school textbook, Trench's *The History of Words,* from which he learned among other things that "dilapidation" comes from "dis" and "lapis, lapidis," and means the falling or removal of stones from a wall.

What I am suggesting is that we stop underestimating our students and make the necessary effort to arouse in them an emotional concern for clarity and precision—if possible, even a passion for clarity and precision. For at the moment all the passion seems to be on the other side. We face what my wife calls a raging fire of unreason: a hatred of all that we and our discipline stand for, a terrible emotional need to destroy thought as the enemy of feeling, deliberation as the enemy of action, and liberal reform as a deception, a means of avoiding significant change. The Supreme Court's unhappy phrase "with all deliberate speed" has in fact been used as an excuse for indecent deliberation in ending a policy that ruins people's lives, a deliberate policy of ruining people's lives; and the indecent deliberators, falsely identifying everything decent with Communism, have in fact been driving more and more of those who oppose racism into the welcoming and constraining arms of Moscow's and Peking's agents—who, alas, are themselves racists, whether by conviction or from opportunism is of no importance. More and more of our students are beginning to fight racism with racism, repression with repression, unreason with unreason, befuddlement with befuddlement. We must not permit ourselves to be pushed like them into the intolerable position of having to choose between Strom Thurmond and LeRoi Jones, for such a dilemma invites mental breakdown. We must try unceasingly to rescue them from it.

Theoretically our colleagues in science and technology should defend and promote intellectual clarity, but actually there is no reason to believe that a majority of them will; theoretically we in the humanities should also defend and promote the qualities that distinguish our species from those that act without thinking, but actually there is no reason to believe that the majority of us will. In any crisis, most of us turn out to be morally timid. It therefore remains for us of the rational, humane and unintimidated minority, not only in English but in all the other disciplines as well, to defend civilization in our own ways and with our own weapons as long as we can. Let us remember, moreover, a lesson from *Finnegans Wake:* that it was not the raffish Gracehoper but the well-barbered Ondt, a genteel opportunist ready to join in whatever tendency seemed most likely to prevail, who said, "What a zeit for the goths!" [*FW* 415.26.] Then, if civilization does go down in incoherence, we will have no cause to feel guilty. We will have defended it to the last unsplit infinitive.

As for the Ondt, his politic defection to the goths with their populist "relevance" will do him no good. For when some glue-sniffing baggage handler puts his suitcase on the wrong plane once too often, or some error-prone computer once too often threatens to sue for payment of a bill he has already paid, he will get an ulcer. His doctor, knowing no physiology because he prescribed his own relevant curriculum of groovy courses and hired his own dreamy teachers, will diagnose it as . . . you know, like appendicitis. The Ondt will then be taken, in like an ambulance thrown together by drop-out mechanics high on pot, toward like a bridge built by theosophical engineers innocent of math, physics and the strength of materials, on the other side of which are like a hospital designed by freaked-out architects who majored in psychedelic design and forgot to put in elevators, and like a hashish-smoking surgeon who knows no anatomy.

# The Shuffling
# Speech of Slavery:
# Black English

As a professor of English in a large urban university surrounded by black slums, I am up against a current form of the romanticism that recurrently softens the human brain: a demand that Black English ("I goes, you goes, he go") be recognized as an effective medium for intellectual work.

The demand has two different motives and takes two different forms, defensive and offensive. The defensive motive is the painful desire of black students to be accepted as they are, without straightening their hair or bleaching their skin: they don't want to change their language either. They think Black English is as natural as the Afro hairdo; but this is a tragic delusion, as we shall see. The offensive motive is the desire of the bitterest among them to reverse the process of linguistic assimilation: to make the white colleges and universities assimilate to them by adopting Black English as a language of instruction, equal though in practice probably separate, and accepting oral and written Black English from black students in all courses. This is a furious assertion of their outraged human dignity, against a society that systematically and explicitly denied it, by statute and by clearly recognized custom, for more than three hundred years, and that still to a large extent retains the assumptions by which it tried to justify slavery.

I leave out of account those students, black and white, who identify with the Third World and want to destroy this one, and who therefore oppose everything indiscriminately: who oppose as racism the universities' exclusive acceptance of standard English, but who if Black English were accepted would oppose the acceptance as racism. I have heard one say in a public speech, to applause and cheers, "If they meet all our demands today, we'll change our minds on 'em tomorrow." To the extent that the demand for Black English comes from people with this attitude it is not a serious demand, and to answer their arguments would be to play their game and beclown onself. But the other two motives are serious, and the arguments that proceed from them must be seriously answered.

The psychological problem that many black students have with standard English is a peculiarly exacerbated variety of the psychological problem that many white students have with standard English; and the exacerbation is so extreme that the difference in degree becomes a difference of kind. Their efforts to cope with it are accordingly different, and our approach to it must be different.

What is standard English? As we all know, the pronunciation of English words differs from country to country, region to region, city to city, neighborhood to neighborhood, social class to social class, and time to time: in eighteenth-century upper-class London, "join" rhymed with "fine," and "tea" with "obey," but the same pronunciations now are lower class. Even in written English there are national differences of spelling, vocabulary, and sometimes grammar. Richard Robinson has observed (in *Definition,* Oxford, 1954, p. 53) that the words "robin" and "sycamore" signify different kinds of birds and trees in different places: that's why we need fancy Latin designations, each attached to a precise and detailed description in a book or learned journal and recorded in an index to such books and journals. In England—God, reason and nature notwithstanding—collective nouns such as "government" and "committee" are treated as plurals—"Her Majesty's government are not prepared to enter the Common Market on these terms"; "the committee have submitted their report." Englishmen generally write "recognise," "botanise" and "economise," ignoring or defying their own *Oxford English Dictionary,* which says that the American suffix -ize is both etymologically and phonetically preferable; they generally write "honour," "labour," "demeanour," "endeavour," "candour," "rancour," "humour" and "rumour," but "pallor," "horror" and "terror," preferring in most but not all cases the Old French to the Latin ending. Moreover, they sometimes don't know the right names of things: they call suspenders "braces," and garters "suspenders"; with equal perversity they call the top of a car the "hood," and the hood the "bonnet." They sometimes get their idioms wrong too, saying "Not to worry" for "Don't worry," and "Cheerio" for "So long."

But all these and all such differences are exceptions. Most of the words in the English vocabulary have the same meanings throughout the English-speaking world; most of them are spelled the same way throughout the English-speaking world; and the grammar of written English is largely uniform throughout the English-speaking world. French publishers do, to be sure, distinguish between books *"traduit de l'anglais"* and *"traduit de l'américain,"* and there is an amusing book entitled *Let Stalk Strine* [Let's Talk Australian], which is full of seeming unintelligibilities. (I seem to have lent it to somebody, but I recall one question: "Emma Chizzit?" means "How much is it?") Even so, readers of English throughout the world can read books written in England, America, Australia, Africa, India or wherever, with little or no difficulty, because written English is largely standard in its grammar, spelling and vocabulary. Now we can answer the question with which the previous paragraph began. Standard English is the English in which most of the books, magazines and newspapers we read are written. The ability to read, write and speak it is a necessary key to the information and artistry books contain and the conversation they make possible.

One of the clichés educationists live by is that the spoken English of the educated classes is called "standard" as a matter of snobbery. But that is a half-truth. Obviously there is snobbery; but the spoken English of the educated classes is called "standard" also because in its grammar and vocabulary it conforms to the world-wide uniformities of written English: in a word, because it *is* standard. Deviations are found chiefly in the speech of people who read little or not at all. In west central Pennsylvania, for example, the usual meanings of

the words "leave" and "let" are regularly reversed by most people: a
passenger says to the bus driver, "Leave me out at the next corner,"
and at a PTA meeting I attended the grammar school principal said,
"I'll just let these-here forms on the table an you kin pickemup at
the end of the meetn." In such communities adults who speak and
write standard English, and who have children, must choose one of
four courses: (1) they can avoid being misfits by adapting their
language to that of the environment and encouraging their children
to do likewise—reversing the usual meanings of "leave" and "let,"
pronouncing "piano" "pie-yanner" and "zebra" "zebray," saying
"The lawrn needs mowed," "The cor needs worshed," "The baby
needs batht," "The horses needs fed," "The bills needs paid," "The
niggers needs kept in their place," "What church does yoons go to?"
etc., etc., alas, etc.; (2) they can make a politic partial adaptation,
speaking one language at home and another in public, incidentally
saying one thing and thinking another, and incurring, they and their
children, whatever twists and curlicues of the psyche may result
from habitually speaking with a forked tongue; (3) they can choose
to be linguistically maladjusted in that little world, and have their
children maladjusted too; (4) they can leave—pardon me, I mean
they can let that little world behind and enter or re-enter the larger
world.

White students from such communities, encountering the larger
world for the first time at a college or university, have psychological
problems of the same kind, but turned in the opposite direction:
suddenly or gradually it dawns on them that if they are to succeed in
the larger world—specifically, if they are to be employable outside
their home communities—and immediately, in the shorter term, if
they are to understand the books they have to read, and engage in
the classroom discussions they are expected to engage in, they will
have to learn a—Well, no. Not a foreign language. That is a different
matter. A foreigner in a strange country *wants* to learn the language,
*wants* to speak it correctly, and makes every effort to speak and
write it as well as he can. He doesn't feel that he is betraying his
native language or culture by becoming proficient in another; on the
contrary, his bilingualism and biculturalism are sources of pride and
pleasure to him: having two angles of vision instead of one, he has

deepened his understanding of many human things—he even understands his own language and culture better than he did before. But our bewildered and culture-shocked college freshman finds that he must learn not a foreign language but the language of another social class in his own country—the presumably superior language of a presumably superior class. This is never flatly stated, but it is insistently implied in the requirement that he give up his familiar native locutions, which he is flatly told are "wrong." Naturally he resents and resists the requirement.

For of course his native locutions are not wrong. For purposes of communication, in his native community, they are right, and standard English is wrong; but since the territory within which they are right is limited, and the territory within which standard English is right is worldwide, and since moreover no books or magazines at all, and no newspapers outside his native community, are written in his native idiom, he must develop some acquaintance with standard English if he is to get through college.

The statement "The territory within which standard English is right is worldwide" needs some qualification. It may well be that in any given community—or in every single community throughout the world—the people who speak and write standard English are a minority. I know beyond question that they are a very tiny minority in Altoona, Pa., where we lived for three years; they may be a comparably tiny minority in Hoboken, N. J., or Astoria, N. Y., or Detroit, Mich., or Billings, Mont., or Boise, Ida., or Walla Walla, Wash., or Dallas, Tex., or Jackson, Miss., or Gloucester, Mass.; but members of that minority in all these cities speak the same language, with minor and unimportant variations, whereas the various local majoritarians, though they could doubtless communicate if they met, would doubtless be inclined to laugh at each other's pronunciation and would from time to time be baffled by outlandish—literally outlandish—differences of idiom. What would the Jacksonian make, for example, of the Altoonan's "She taken a scunner to me"? And how would the Hobokener know that the Jacksonian's "gyowry" meant "porch"?

The psychological effect of discovering that one's native idiom is an off-brand of limited distribution, and is regarded as inferior by

one's teachers, and is not to be found in one's textbooks, and worst
of all is proscribed, is shocking—especially if one has always
belonged to an unquestioned majority and has always been
culturally hostile to anything unfamiliar. The difficulty that many
freshmen have with standard English is thus less intellectual than
psychological. But we cannot let them refuse to learn standard
English, because with their limited vocabularies, many of whose
words are merely local or regional, and their unfamiliarity with the
standard grammar of world-wide English, they cannot understand
the books they will have to read, or discuss them orally or in writing
with any fluency or precision, or be capable of having ideas that
their neighbors "down home" are not linguistically equipped to
have. Unavoidably, with the best of democratic intentions, we ask
them to grow beyond their native culture and alienate themselves
from their neighbors, friends and relatives. Unavoidably, with the
best of democratic intentions, we ask them to identify with people
they have always considered effete impudent snobs. (Incidentally,
when they say "impudent" they mean "insolent." Whether Mr.
Agnew was wrong deliberately or unintentionally is a nice but futile
question.)

Most of our white students, however, unlike most of our black
students, were not seriously alienated *before* they came to college;
and many of them go complacently through to an unalienated
graduation. Look around you. On most campuses the Raskolnikov
look and the Jesus Christ look, with their corresponding versions of
Sonia and Mary Magdalen, are cultivated by two overlapping
minorities, or four if you prefer, which taken together are still
a minority; and many of these are just playing at poverty like Marie
Antoinette, or wearing theatrical costumes, or being fashionable in
their group, or living fantasy lives. Appearance is by no means a
reliable guide to mentality: some of the most independent thinkers
are quite conventional in appearance, and some of the tamest are
frowzy-headed. In the world of the tame all is well: God's in His
heaven, Efferdent's bubbles are scrubbing away at stain and odor,
Canada Dry tastes like love, and Standard Oil doesn't pollute the air
or water. They really think we have liberty and justice for all; they
really think the police are dedicated to impartial apolitical main-

tenance of law and order; and it never occurs to them that when the President of the United States announces an all-out crusade for some good social purpose he is announcing a cutback of funds, a reduction of staff, a closing of facilities and a cancellation of programs devoted to that purpose, together with the dismissal or transfer of all officials who in their naive apolitical good will actually wanted to achieve it.

But black students know better. Through long experience—their own, their families' and their friends'—they know that they may at any time be arbitrarily arrested or spontaneously beaten up, for no cause other than some white or black policeman's personal neurosis or perversion or disappointment or high spirits, and that society affords them neither protection nor redress—whether from indifference or by deliberate policy makes no practical difference. And, having observed the reduction or non-implementation of housing, health and job-training programs that might have helped them, they know what the word "crusade" means. Every black student with whom I have spoken is completely skeptical of official statements. But then so am I, for the present and as far into the future as I can now see, and so are many of my friends, colleagues and acquaintances, regardless of race. What is peculiar to many black students—an increasing many—is the belief that all whites are racists and that white society acts as a centrally directed organization to keep them in an inferior status. When one agency of government draws up a program of job training, for example, and another agency, such as the White House, reduces it to an advertising display designed by the Potemkins on its staff, our black students tend to accuse the first agency as well as the second of bad faith and to lump both together as "Whitey." They don't believe there is any apolitical good will; they have long since given up any apolitical good will they themselves may have had, as a foolishness they can't afford; and every day's newspapers bring additional news that the official leaders of white society have once again confirmed them in that view.

Growing numbers of them now believe that the colleges' use of standard English as the only language of instruction (outside of advanced foreign language courses) is just another white trick to keep them down; they regard the colleges' insistence that they learn to express themselves in standard English as a manifestation of racism. They consider Black English a perfectly satisfactory medium of communication, which moreover is intelligible to whites as well as blacks. Why, therefore, if not because of racial prejudice, is it not accepted as a legitimate language for term papers, theses and dissertations?

Because it is not a satisfactory medium for the communication of precise information or the development of clear ideas. Literate black leaders of the eighteenth and nineteenth centuries—Benjamin Banneker, Frederick Douglass, John Russworm, and all the others without exception—spoke and wrote eloquent standard English; and in the twentieth century Black English has seldom been the spoken language and never the written language (except by way of quotation and fictional dialogue) of any black leader, be he or she a novelist, a playwright, a poet, a teacher, a historian, an economist, a sociologist, a public official, a doctor, a lawyer, a publicist or a revolutionary. Who among these can't or couldn't or doesn't or didn't write standard English?—Ralph Abernathy, James Baldwin, Julian Bond, Arna Bontemps, Ralph Bunche, Margaret Butcher, George Cannon, Shirley Chisholm, Eldridge Cleaver, Price Cobbs, Angela Davis, W. E. B. DuBois, Ralph Ellison, Charles Evers, Medgar Evers, Kenneth Gibson, Dick Gregory, William Grier, Lorraine Hansbury, George Jackson, Helen Johnson, LeRoi Jones, Martin Luther King, Alain Locke, Thurgood Marshall, Gerald McWorter, Willard Motley, Robert Moton, Huey Newton, L. D. Reddick, J. Saunders Redding, Bayard Rustin, Carl Stokes, Darwin Turner, Roy Wilkins, Richard Wright, Malcolm X. On the other hand, can the advocates of Black English name one black leader or spokesman with more than a neighborhood following who habitually expresses himself in Black English?

It doesn't lend itself to clear expression. It was the language of slavery. It was taught to illiterate slaves by illiterate overseers, whose language it was. Of course the slave owners didn't object to its inadequacy for intellectual communication; they were amused, not distressed, by the imprecision of their slaves' thought. Before the Civil War all Southern states had laws making it illegal to teach slaves to read and write, and no Southern states had public schools for whites until after the Civil War, because they didn't want the slaves or the poor whites to acquire information or develop ideas or to be able to present clearly and forcefully such information and ideas as they might have. The conservative opposition to integrated schools springs from fear that the races may become less easy to play off against each other; conservatives are quite right to fear "uppity niggers" who speak clearly and eloquently; they much prefer Black English, a language of imprecision, the heritage of slavery. And alas, for many blacks it has the appeal of the familiar, of custom and easy continuity, of shuffling on in the same old way.

Moses had some difficulty making the ancient Jews give up the habits of slavery. They kept wanting to go back to Egypt. "Are you hankering for the easy life you had, the good times and the fleshpots?" he sneered. Finally he gave up: it dawned on him, or maybe one night in his tent he read it in Rousseau's *Social Contract* I.2, that a man born in slavery is born for slavery: that if he adjusts to it well enough to survive he destroys his will and loses his self-respect and no longer has the spirit to act as a free man. All powerlessness corrupts, and absolute powerlessness corrupts absolutely. So he just marched them around in the desert for forty years of impotent vagabondage, allowing two and a half generations for the customs of slavery to die out with the slaves. Then those who had grown up in freedom seized their freedom. The different conditions of black life in America, notably the physical impossibility of exodus, and the ninety years—the five or six generations—of systematic suppression backed by organized terror, that followed the Civil War, have retarded the development of black freedom and encouraged the perpetuation of the old demoralized ways. Black English is demoralized language, an idiom of fettered minds, the shuffling speech of slavery. It served its bad purposes well. It cannot serve the purposes of free men and women. Those who would perpetuate it are romanticists clinging to corruption.

## *Appendix: An Exchange of Letters*

In accepting this article for publication in *College English,* the editor, Richard Ohmann, wrote me the following letter. In subsequent correspondence we agreed that it would be interesting to publish his letter and my reply in the magazine. They will appear in a future issue.

Dear Mr. Morse:

We want to publish your article, but hope that you will clear up a couple of points for us, if you agree that they could use clarification.

Your divorcing standard English from snobbery makes good sense, but shouldn't you also divorce it from the phonological side of regional dialects? The people who talk standard English in Boston sound very different from their counterparts in New Orleans, but no one tries to eradicate the differences in school, and we don't think you mean that they should. Yet you talk of pronunciation along with idiom and grammar. Is the fact that some pronounce "piano" "pie-yanner" any more pertinent to your case than the fact that JFK pronounced "idea" "idear"? And is the difference between JFK's linguistic situation and that of a working class or black student more than that JFK had the power and status to talk with confidence as he damn well pleased? And if so, shouldn't English teachers throw more of their energies into changing the social situation than into changing black dialect?

We also wonder about your criticism of localisms like "gyowry" and "scunner." Some at least of such idiosyncrasies are welcomed as expressive and flavorful, even in some college writing courses. How do you distinguish between those expressions that are accepted and those that, because they impede communication or stigmatize the speaker, should be avoided? And does it make a difference whether these expressions appear in speech or in writing? Isn't it relatively easy for speakers of different dialects to clear up misunderstandings when they are face to face?

Thank you for letting us publish the article.

Sincerely, Richard Ohmann

Dear Mr. Ohmann:

I agree, up to a point. We should no more expect or want people to talk alike than we should expect or want them to look alike. We don't and shouldn't discourage localisms or regionalisms unless, as you put it, "they impede communication or stigmatize the speaker"—but "scunner" and "gyowry" (gallery) do impede communication in most of the English-speaking world, and such pronunciations are "pie-yanner" and "idear" do stigmatize the speaker, even JFK, outside the limited areas where they are current. (Proust observed that the Duchesse de Guermantes and the illiterate servant Françoise spoke the same antique regional French—*A la recherche du temps perdu*, Pléiade edition, II, 34 ff.; in the same passage he observed that servants from different regions of France could hardly understand each other.) I would add that localisms, regionalisms and classisms should be avoided if they impede thought or study. A person who has difficulty with the agreement of subject and verb can't think clearly; and a person whose habitual way of expressing such agreement differs from the standard way must suffer a disadvantage when he comes to read a book.

Moreover, we should beware of the picturesque as a handle for condescension, and of self-conscious picturesqueness as a way of catering to condescension; and we should be aware that the promotion of folksiness goes hand in hand with political reaction. See, for example, T. S. Eliot's recommendations on this subject in *Notes Towards the Definition of Culture* and *The Idea of a Christian Society*. Those who oppose what they call "cosmopolitanism" in culture are without exception reactionary in politics.

But my article is concerned chiefly with the practical effects of Black English on the lives of those who speak it. Our anthropologist friends tell us there are class differences in speech throughout the world, and I have been given a saddening insight into one practical effect those differences have on college students in two other countries. As a Fulbright lecturer, I spent the academic year 1964–65 teaching American literature at the University of Toulouse. In Toulouse, as throughout southern France, there is a Spanish influence on the speech of those not born in what Jacques Barzun calls the House of Intellect. Our neighborhood grocer, instead of saying "Dix francs, quarante-cinq centimes," said "Dix-a franca, quaranta-cinqua centima"; and when a pregnant woman got on a crowded bus the ticket-seller would call out, "Plaça pour una dama enceinta, s'il vous plaît." No matter how crowded the bus, the woman always had her choice of two or three seats—it was wonderful; still, the ticket-seller's language is not standard French; and many English majors at the university, who had learned to speak perfect Oxonian English, were hindered in their careers because they had continued to speak their native French with a Spanish accent. It was and is, alas, a class indicator. The French and British governments have an exchange arrangement whereby some of the best French students majoring in English spend a year in England as resource people and assistant teachers in high school French classes, and some of the best British students majoring in French spend a year in France as resource people and assistant teachers in high school English classes: I met the visiting British educational official who was screening candidates at Toulouse; he told me sadly that he had to reject some highly intelligent students, who spoke excellent English, because they spoke lower-class Toulousain French; and a member of the English Department at the University of Toulouse said, "We likewise reject British students who speak with a Cockney accent."

Before we attribute this practice to mere snobbery, we should ask ourselves if we would want our own children to enter the job market saddled with Cockney English or a regional variety of lower-class French. Those who want black students to continue to be saddled with an analogous handicap should at least be conscious of what it is they are asking for.

But there is a much more serious handicap. Everybody who has ever corrected freshman themes knows that a limited vocabulary and a limited command of syntax limit the possibilities of thought; and that an inaccurate vocabulary and an unreliable command of syntax often shipwreck thought. Black English, like silent-majority white English, lacks the vocabulary and the syntactic resources for thought of even moderate complexity. I doubt that the following paragraph from Marx's *Capital,* for example, can be translated into Black English; I know beyond question that people whose vocabulary and syntax are limited to those of Black English—or of silent-majority white English—cannot possibly understand it:

In proportion as exchange bursts its local bonds, the character of money attaches itself to commodities that are by nature fitted to perform the social function of a universal equivalent. Those commodities are the precious metals. If money is to equate every other commodity to any amount, and thus to represent any exchange-value that may be wished for, a material is needed whose every sample exhibits the same uniform qualities. On the other hand, since the difference between the magnitudes of value is purely quantitative, the money commodity must be divisible at will, and equally capable of being reunited. Gold and silver possess these properties by nature.

The pleasures of rich, complex and sophisticated literary beauty are likewise inaccessible within the lexical and syntactic limits of black or silent-majority white English. Consider this sentence from Saint Augustine's *The City of God:* "To Him, through solemn feasts and on appointed days, we consecrate the memory of His benefits, lest through the lapse of time ungrateful oblivion should steal upon us." I reject Saint Augustine's religious, political and social ideas, but his prose delights me. I enjoy it where I live—in my body, with my blood. I don't think with my blood, however. The value of this sentence is not intellectual but aesthetic—a value created by its rhythms, its periodic suspensions, its intuitively perceived firmness of structure; translate them away—say, for example, "We has these big holiday dinner so we won't forget how good God been to us"—and its beauty evaporates. Those who lack language to enjoy it suffer a real deprivation.

The passage from Marx has intellectual but no aesthetic value; the one from Saint Augustine has aesthetic but no intellectual value. The greatest writing—e.g., Proust's—has both; the worst—e.g., such commercial fakery as Edgar Guest's "It takes a heap o' livin' / To make a house a home"—has neither. But people who lack linguistic equipment have little or no protection against the ludicrous metaphors ("heap"), the condescension ("o' livin' ") and the cliché sentimentalities of commercial fakery. They are almost helplessly drawn to writing that makes no intellectual demands and offers no disturbing aesthetic stimulation, but affords only a kind of analgesic escape from vacancy, such as—to quote Coleridge—"gaming, swinging on a chair or a gate; spitting over a bridge; smoking; snuff-taking; tête-à-tête quarrels after dinner between husband and wife; conning word by word all the advertisements of the *Daily Advertizer* in a public house on a rainy day, etc. etc. etc." (*Biographia Literaria*, chapter III, note 1 or 2, depending on the edition.) George Orwell had a word for it: "prolefeed." In capitalist countries, if only it promotes the kind of morality that regards sex as immoral and the suppression of civil liberaties as moral, we call it Worthwhile Reading or Wholesome Literature; in Communist countries, if only it promotes the same kind of morality, they call it Socialist Realism. Its political equivalent is peddled by authoritarians everywhere, in varieties that differ only as one soap opera differs from another. The titles differ, the scenario is always the same. Mao tse-Tung calls it "The New Culture"; Brezhnev calls it "Soviet Virtue"; Nixon calls it "A Driving Dream"; George Wallace, who used to call it "Run Over 'em!", now needs a new title; William F. Buckley, Jr. (George Wallace pretending to be Robert de Montesquiou) calls it "Human Nature"! They all fear precise language and precise information; they all fear us unimpressed intellectuals. They wish we would stop encouraging students to be critical—to think. They'd like to silence us, or put us in jail, or even kill us. Mao and Brezhnev, who can, do.

I don't buy the cheap popular superstition, whose hawkers have now updated their spiel by replacing the Biblical quotations with statistics, that blacks are innately incapable of complex thought or of responding to complex beauty: but as a teacher I am painfully aware that many black and silent-majority white students lack the linguistic keys that would open to them the world of complex thought and complex beauty. The keys cannot be acquired without effort, on their part and on ours. I ask all students and all teachers, regardless of race, to make the effort. We must not silently let our students accept, as many of them do accept, the reactionary notion that they are innately incapable of successful intellectual effort. We must encourage them to reject the notion, if only because in some cases it tends to be self-confirming. That is how we, *as English teachers,* can work to change a repressive society into one that must respect personal freedom. Which doesn't prevent us, *as citizens,* from working in other ways to change it. I see no contradiction between helping students to become articulate and working for social change;

in fact, I doubt that linguistically hobbled students can help to bring about any but reactionary change.

Sincerely yours, J. Mitchell Morse

P.S. My son Jonathan, a graduate student of English at Indiana University, to whom I have sent copies of the article and the ensuing correspondence, writes in reply as follows:

In a good book with a bad title, Samuel Putnam's memoir of the literary life of the 1920's, *Paris Was Our Mistress* (Viking, 1947), there's a kind of objective correlative of the class and language situation you describe. In 1930 or so, Putnam says, he and his family were living among expatriate artists and writers in Mirmande, an isolated medieval village (population 125), in Southern France. The economic situation, however, and the new emphasis on social consciousness in literature, made him and his wife think of returning to the United States. Besides, "our children . . . were growing up speaking only French, and not even good French, but a patois which the village four miles away, with a patois of its own, did not understand. It was all right, perhaps, for our generation to be 'lost,' but had we any right to 'lose' another?" [1]

The epiphanic moment of decision came one day when Putnam, watching the picturesque European peasant plowing with picturesque traditional oxen just below his window, heard a noise, looked up, saw the *Graf Zeppelin* directly overhead on its weekly voyage out of the heart of Europe, and realized that realities succeed each other: to look back is always futile or worse.

Of course we all yearn for authenticity: it's why most of us go to see *Shaft* or *Fiddler on the Roof*, it's why we allow every provincial fraud in the United States to convince us that he knows some deep wisdom we don't. (For a horrible example, see *Foxfire* magazine, with its picture stories about picturesque Georgia mountaineers, all apostrophes, talking their way through—no kidding—explanations of how to wash clothes in a creek or make an ox yoke.) But there's no such thing as authenticity. The sky is too full of zeppelins. Ultimately, we're all cultural missionaries, whether we want to be or not; let's not pretend that we want the natives to stay as they are. That way lie the reservations.

---

1. Copyright © 1947 by The Viking Press. Reprinted by permission.

# Literature as Subversion

The Snopesian quality of the Nixon administration is nowhere more evident than in its sour antagonism to college students and teachers, whom Nixon, Agnew and Mitchell quite rightly consider dangerous to everything they stand for—and perhaps, though this is necessarily a matter of conjecture, to all they personally are. But I am concerned less with their psychological difficulties than with our own; for they have many unwitting allies among us liberal intellectuals, who, far from regarding the humanities as dangerous, are turning away from them as irrelevant. The following remarks are addressed to these people of good will—teachers, students, sympathizers.

Relevance involves a concern with current issues and with many other things as well, such as the processes of thought and feeling and the validity of choices and values; and our concern with these other things—without which our concern with current issues would be superficial and subject to all kinds of demagogic appeals—is often expressed in metaphors. In the middle ages the question "How many angels can dance on the point of a needle?" never came up. It was first suggested in 1678, by the anti-scholastic Ralph Cudworth, to illustrate what he considered the irrelevance of the schoolmen's intellectual interests. But Duns Scotus, the eponymous alleged father of all such dunceries, seldom discussed angels, and when he did he discussed questions of a much more serious kind—such as "Can an angel be in more than one place at the same time?" "Can more angels than one be in the same place at the same time?" "When an angel moves from one place to another, does any time elapse?" and "Can an angel move from one place to another without passing through the intervening space?" He discussed such questions because students asked them, at weekly sessions where they were permitted to ask whatever they pleased—in fact, the title of the book from which I have just quoted them is *Quaestiones Quodlibetales* [Free Questions]. His answers indicate that he was discussing questions that are still asked in modern philosophy because they have to do with intellectual clarity: Are there entities that are not physical? If so, can we think of them as occupying space and time? If we can't think of them in such terms, how can we conceive them at all? In speaking of them, can we legitimately use spatial and temporal terms even as metaphors? The problem of ineffability still exercises our modern logicians. The Clerk of Oxenford and his fellow students sat at the feet of John Wyclif (a man deeply involved in current religio-political issues), read Duns Scotus and William of Ockham with him, and didn't consider them irrelevant. These thinkers were in fact concerned less with angels than with the nature of the church and of the individual and of the right relations between them: they built the metaphysical foundations of the theory of Protestant individualism, which itself underlies the theory of representative government.

But the new interests, new emphases and new metaphors of the Renaissance made them seem irrelevant. Milton, who was hardly an anti-intellectual, regarded with contempt all their metaphysics, whose relevance escaped him—"Vain wisdom all, and false Philosophie." And whether through contempt or through actual ignorance, he appeared to know nothing of angelology. He called Satan, who as Lucifer in Heaven had been second only to God, the lost archangel; he called Beelzebub a fallen cherub; he had the fallen cherub respectfully address the lost archangel as leader of the embattled seraphim. That was like having a colonel respectfully address a corporal as leader of the embattled generals.

As a professor of English at a large urban university surrounded by black slums, I often wonder what the hell I am doing. Is the study of literature to go the way of angelology? Should it? Will even the most learned men of the future find it irrelevant, vain, false and contemptible? How important is literary scholarship to a family living in a leaky building infested with rats? How important are the things we do in this pleasant white enclave? Consider, for example, one of the favorite scholarly activities of us English teachers, the tracing of literary influences. In *The Dream Life of Balso Snell* (*The Collected Works of Nathanael West,* Farrar, Strauss & Giroux, p. 27) there is a brief passage on laughter. In Samuel Beckett's *Watt* (Grove Press, p. 48) there is a somewhat longer and much more brilliant passage on laughter. In view of certain obvious correspondences between the two passages, and in view of the fact that there are other correspondences between the two novels, and in view of the fact that *Watt* was published 22 years after *The Dream Life of Balso Snell,* we might infer that Beckett was "influenced" by West as well as by Aristotle, whose face also shows through the passage. But what is the value of that inference? Quite aside from its irrelevance to the immediate problem of doing something about those leaky buildings and the ruined lives in them, does it have any value that relates to the art of writing? Does it help us to understand either Beckett or West? The important thing about an artist is not where he gets his material but what he does with it. Since we cannot attribute the quality of Shakespeare's art in the histories to Holinshed's *Chronicles,* the fact that Shakespeare found material in Holinshed is of only incidental interest. Joyce found material—including anecdotes—in Thom's *Dublin Directory;* Proust found material in the gossip of waiters. To say that Shakespeare was "influenced" by Holinshed,or Joyce by Thom, or Proust by Olivier of the Ritz, is even misleading: it tempts us to believe that we understand what we may very well not understand.

Nevertheless, we academics who profess literature are accustomed to justifying our lives in part by the alleged value of such studies—not only for the education of future writers but for all our fellow men and women, whether or not they are aware of it. Truth, we say: the never-ending discovery of Truth, a universal value in and of itself; and since the interconnections of its infinite details are infinite, one detail is as indispensable as another and all truths are equally valuable; there is, moreover, a moral value in the disciplined effort of seeking them out, and perhaps ultimately (you never know) a practical application as well. The practical applications of the humanities turn out to be moral maxims to the effect that those who know no history are doomed to repeat it and that everybody is somehow improved by acquaintance with the best that has been thought and said and that lives of great men all remind us we can make our lives subliminal and departing leave behind us footprints of a nut or criminal.

Few of us take such arguments seriously any more, if we ever did take them as seriously as in our defensive earnestness we pretended to. We know as well as any historian that historians are not exempt from the general doom, and as well as any statesman or politician that they don't necessarily make good statesmen or good politicians; we know as well as any well-paid electronic engineer that a knowledge of literature is not necessary for the successful conduct of outer life; we know as well as any intellectually prancing symbolic logician that it is not necessary for a joyful inner life; and when we read the scholarly journals devoted to literature we are painfully reminded that it doesn't guarantee that we will write well or even be good judges of writing. So what good is it? How can we justify the time we spend on it?

The other humanities are in the same case; but this fact may point toward an answer. We know from our own experience and observation that a knowledge of symbolic logic is not necessary either for the successful conduct of outer life or for a rich inner life, and that those who have it are not thereby guaranteed to write logically or even to think logically in ordinary unsymbolic situations; analogous things can be said about history, philology, metaphysics, etc.: no knowledge of any one of the humanities is necessary. But surely a knowledge of some one of them is necessary? No. I have friends who know nothing of literature, history, logic, metaphysics or any other of the humanities, but who are quite successful in their outer lives and happy in their inner lives and effective for good in all their human relations and as contemptuous of Spiro Agnew as you or I. However valuable or even necessary the humanities may be for civilized society, they are not necessary for any individual. As personal possessions or attainments, they have no value except the exercises in pleasure they afford us. They are the dancing of the mind.

And that is ample justification for them. A life confined to useful activities and physical necessities, a life without pleasure, is not worth living: it is the life of a beast of burden, a slave or a prisoner: something more, something free, undirected and uncalculated, something beyond mere animal survival, some gratuitous activity, some non-utilitarian gentle or ecstatic pleasure, is necessary for a tolerable human life; every man chooses within the limits of his purse and the inclinations of his personality the pleasures that suit him, and we who enjoy pleasures of an intellectual kind need not apologize to anyone, least of all to anti-intellectual demagogues who find conditioned reflexes more manageable than the free intelligence that is the peculiar mark of humanity, and who therefore, in their well-founded fear of the intelligence of the governed, regard us teachers of the humanities with suspicion and ill will. We who would not deny to others their external pleasures have a moral duty—I will even go so far as to say a patriotic duty—to defend our internal pleasures; for if we lose the right to enjoy Valery Larbaud's prose with our beer, on that day no man will be secure in the right to enjoy beer with his beer.

In the dictatorships to our right and left there is direct and undisguised censorship of ideas; the bourgeois democracies, being somewhat more sophisticated, are less afraid of ideas than of art. By this I don't mean that the Nixon administration is not afraid of ideas, but only that a certain irreducible sophistication inheres in our Constitution. In the democracies a writer can say anything without officially alarming the censors, if he doesn't say it well. Our censors know, if only instinctively, that trash is never subversive: that Nabokov's apolitical but well-written *Lolita* is more dangerous to the authoritarianism they love than any vulgar pornographic novel, or than Katherine Anne Porter's poorly written anti-fascist *Ship of Fools.* Our censorship is hardly ever political, and seldom moral; it is chiefly aesthetic. The one thing a conservative bourgeois fears more than anything else is literary brilliance. To be sure, the Nixon administration crudely tried to prevent *The New York Times* from discrediting the official lies by publishing the official documents on the war in Vietnam, and its Vice-President has crudely threatened a general political censorship of editorial comment; but even if the press were more timidly vapid than it is in discussing public issues the effect of such censorship would be slight, because there isn't much farther to go in the direction of vapidity; though there are exceptions, the large majority of newspapers, magazines and TV programs have never had any trouble living down to the intellectual standards of the advertising agencies they depend on and the demagogues they fear.

A subtler and more serious threat to the quality of our life inheres in the recent revival of federal interest in pornography. In the modern urban world pornography has almost always been as widely available as sex itself, and the laws against it have most often been used not to close the porno shops or remove the skin magazines from your friendly neighborhood newsstand or drugstore but to suppress *Flowers of Evil, Madame Bovary, Germinal, Against the Grain, Dubliners, Ulysses, Lady Chatterley's Lover* and other works that by their literary quality invite serious unorthodox thought about the way we live. All experience indicates that if our Attorney General mounts a crusade against pornography, *The Tin Drum* and *The Sound and the Fury* are more liable to be removed from the shelves of public libraries than *Lust Pill, Hot Skin, Wham Bam Gal, Bodies in Heat, Three on a Bed* and *The Lustful Three* from drugstores a block away. (These are actual titles; they are all on display in the store where we pick up our daily *New York Times.* Agnew has threatened the *Times,* but not the publishers of these books.) It isn't sexual stimulation that makes the censors nervous, but intellectual stimulation: and they know that the intellect is stimulated by ideas only to the extent that they are well stated. For the detection of dangerous ideas every censor has an infallible guiding principle: if the prose is good, so that it turns him personally off, he feels in his bones a need to inform the FBI—or, as the case may be, the MVD, since—in Russia as everywhere else—the revolutionary idea, having succeeded to power, has become institu-

tionalized, stuffy and reactionary: our Attorney General in an
inadvertently revealing statement has admitted that he prefers
Communists to liberals: what galls him, even as it galls Brezhnev and
Mao tse-Tung, is the articulacy of free minds.

The most galling thing about a free and articulate mind is the
unlicensed pleasure it takes in its own articulacy: and the most
outrageously joyful exercise of articulacy is the creation of nuances:
I say "creation" rather than "expression," because nuances of
thought and feeling don't exist until we find words to constitute
them. They don't pre-exist like toothpaste in a tube, to be merely
squeezed out or ex-pressed; they are new things that come into being
only when we make them. The ancient Greeks had the right words:
*poiesis,* making, and *poietike,* the process, technique or art of
making. *Making:* not recording, not expressing, not conforming, but
making—devising, constructing, creating.

This is a fundamental revolutionary activity that changes our
ways of thinking and feeling, just as the discovery and application of
scientific principles are fundamental revolutionary activities that
change our economic, social and political arrangements. All such
activities go together to make us increasingly conscious of our lives,
each supporting and supported by the others. When literacy was the
privilege of a minority, censorship was aimed only at the explicit
statement or unmistakable dramatization of unorthodox ideas; the
governing class, having itself been exposed in school to the polite
pleasures of well-made language, did not perceive in such language
the deep springs of originality and hence of unorthodoxy.

But in our more democratic day the danger is more obvious; now
that many people read, our censors and would-be censors not only
attack pornography and explicit unorthodoxy, but in their merely
instinctive and intuitive way they also react with hatred against any
fineness, cleanness or comeliness of language. And these slovenly
demagogues have allies among the artists and intellectuals they
despise and are despised by; in fact, politically conservative artists
and intellectuals preceded the demagogues in opposing the spread of
literacy and the increase of consciousness. Barbey d'Aurevilly called
the Enlightenment a giant earwig that had destroyed the only good
society, the society based on a hereditary order of domination and

submission; Mallarmé deplored the publication of good poetry in cheap editions that made it easily obtainable; Ortega y Gasset regretted the rising employment that made it hard to get good servants, and the rising self-respect that made it necessary to consider their feelings if you wanted to keep them; Aldous Huxley resented the fact that so many people who were neither well born nor well educated nor remarkably virtuous had steam heat and running water to make them proud and lazy; he called for the abolition of public education, and worked to popularize psychedelic drugs; T. S. Eliot said flatly that the masses should be confined from birth in a culture of limited consciousness: i.e., that they should be trained to do mechanical work and imbued with a humbling religion, but not exposed to history, poetry or philosophy, and not forbidden to indulge their superstitions and prejudices; in our own time Hugh Kenner and Marshall McLuhan have attacked the invention of printing and the spread of literacy with arguments that bridge the gap between Barbey d'Aurevilly and the Beatles, those pie-eyed pipers.

The assault on clear consciousness is also joined by many mere innocents, who if they knew their own interests would defend it: I mean those students who in the name of "relevance" would remove Shakespeare, Milton, Swift and Joyce from the curriculum in favor of such dream peddlers as Rod McKuen, Hermann Hesse, Edgar Cayce and Ayn Rand. "Like Shakespeare is irrelevant," one of them told me, "because like you know like he says like 'thee' and 'thou.' " I was reminded of Coleridge's objection to "the unmeaning repetitions, habitual phrases and other blank counters which an unfurnished or confused understanding interposes at short intervals in order to keep hold of his subject which is still slipping from him, and to give him time for recollection; or in mere aid of vacancy." (*Biographia Literaria,* end of chapter XVII—another irrelevant book.)

Thus the enemies of thought attack from all sides—and we English teachers seldom counterattack. We offer very little instruction in writing above the freshman level, and our instruction in literature still deals less with the great writers' artistry than with periods, genres, movements: with literature as a manifestation of

intellectual history, cultural history, economic history, political
history. This is all very well as far as it goes, but it doesn't go very
far toward enabling our students to tell good contemporary writing
from bad, or to judge the quality of a politician's discourse, or to
discourse themselves, in speech or writing, clearly, precisely and
forcefully. The most distressing thing about Agnew's TV debate with
a picked group of college students was that their brains were even
more clogged with clichés than his, so that they couldn't refute his
cheap cynicism or even quite perceive its cheapness. They don't say,
"I think," but "I feel"—and their feeling is non-verbal. Their
utterance therefore doesn't communicate much but vague good will
and warm confusion. Like they can't say what they mean because
like you know like they don't know what they mean because like
you know like they can't say it. With such language, who can think
clearly?

We must help them to clean and tighten and polish and sharpen
their language, making it into a precision instrument that will work.
We must integrate the teaching of literature with the teaching of
writing. Milton, in the *Tractate of Education,* said English composition should come last in the curriculum, not first. He certainly had a
point in his day and for his students; but in our day, and for our
students, composition should come first, last, and all the way
through. Literature and composition should be taught together at all
levels, including the graduate level. Each should be taught as an
aspect of the other—and not as a task, but as part of the pleasure. We
should use the neglected teaching techniques of pastiche and parody.

We will never understand our life if we don't look beneath the
surface of the present, or have much skill with English prose if we
don't experience its possibilities. We must read less ordinary prose
and more artful prose. We must read the most artful writers of the
past and of the present, primarily as masters of technique; and the
best way to understand what they were or are doing is to try to do it
ourselves. A student who has a parodist's familiarity with the devices
of Sir Thomas Browne and Robert Burton and Dr. Johnson and
Carlyle and Dickens and Cardinal Newman and Pater and Wilde and
Hemingway and Faulkner and Beckett has learned to do a number of
things with language, has developed a more than ordinary facility in

using it, and has a strong possibility of being able to achieve a style of his own. Having at his command a variety of syntaxes, cadences and rhetorical games and configurations, he will certainly be a better writer and a clearer thinker than one whose only resources are some rules of textbook grammar (Never End a Sentence with a Preposition), a stock of ready-made phrases (Far out! Groovy!) and a handful of blank counters (like you know like).

Only if we institute some such intellectual anti-poverty program can we subvert the dreary, mean and sordid Snopesism that now disgraces our national life.

# For an
# Articulate
# Majority

How many horse troughs have you seen lately? As I write, the R. J. Reynolds Tobacco Co. is running a TV commercial in which a gang of small-town bullies throw a lone bespectacled unlikely prig into a horse trough because he objects to the bad grammar of a cigarette slogan. "Whaddaya want?" they ask with well-drilled choral spontaneity: "Good grammar, or good taste?" Thus they carry the art of the *non seq.* to its ultimate perfection, demonstrate their moral and political rectitude, and reassure themselves as to their manliness.

We know who they are. One is President of the United States. One is Vice-President. One is Attorney General. The rest are Southern Governors of the type of Wallace and Maddox.

The kind of populism they represent is a much more serious threat to all teachers and students, and to the articulacy we liberal teachers and students stand for, and to personal freedom, and to racial equality, and even to law and order, than is the alleged elitism of which we falsely accuse each other. For their kind of populism— which has almost nothing in common with that of Altgeld and the La Follettes, of Muskie and McGovern and Eugene McCarthy and Ralph Nader and Shirley Chisholm and Julian Bond and the Evers brothers and James E. Chaney and those phony safe Jew-bastard liberals Andrew Goodman and Michael Schwerner[1] —is a kind of inverted elitism based not on individual excellence, which they don't believe in, but on a simple-minded assumption of group superiority: they don't think "I am better than you," but—depending on the local localism—"us is bettern yall" or "Weens is bettern yoons." This is the populism of Enoch Powell and his skinheads in England, of Tixier-Vignancourt and his followers who write "Nègres et bécots, chez vous" and "Mort aux juifs" on walls in France, of l'Uomo Qualunque in Italy, of the National Democrats in Germany, of the Maoist New-Culture mobs in China, of the white-collar rabble who subserve the Ministry of Culture in Russia, and of the Southern Strategists, axe-handle-wielders, flag-worshippers, student-killers and school-bus-wreckers in the United States. These are the people who, though they hate and rightly fear precision of thought and speech, though they have always chosen for their children the cheapest teachers in the market, though they have always prohibited academic freedom as much as possible, now suddenly profess to be concerned lest the intellectual quality of their schools be lowered by the admission of black students. They is hearn tell of that-there Jensen repote, even effen they ain't hearn tell of nothin' else. Not that such intellects are peculiar to the South, or that racism is directed against blacks alone. In the Newark, N.J., mayoral election of 1970 there were undoubtedly many old-line white families, who have been speaking their native English like slobs since 1066 or 597, who felt it was a God-damn shame to hafta choose between a nigger an' a wop. In English cartoons of the Victorian period, Irishmen were always simian. When Joseph Dorfman was gathering material for his life of Thorstein Veblen he went to Wisconsin and Minnesota and interviewed people who had known Veblen, and heard a perfect expression of the racism that Ole Rölvaag had dramatized in the

---

1. Cecil M. Brown thinks of himself as a leftist; but "jew-bastard," "overliterate" and "effete" are three of the eleven right-wing clichés he used, after the violent deaths of Goodman, Schwerner and Mrs. Violet Liuzzo, and the beating and jailing of many others, to describe white liberals—who, he says, don't use their bodies, invest their souls, or risk their lives. See "The White Whale," *Partisan Review,* no. 3, 1969. One of the most unmistakable symptoms of the current intellectual slackness is the detumescence of the *Partisan Review.*

incident of the discharged soldiers in *Giants in the Earth:* an old man told him that the native English speakers had had a saying, "Them Scandahoovians is worse than niggers." That is the voice of racial superiority; the attitude it voices is now, pretty much throughout the world, the most prevalent, most aggressive, most virulent and most destructive form of elitism. After the killing and wounding of black students at Jackson State College, the Attorney General of the United States said he would try to find out what we liberals were "so uptight about."

Elitism assumes that the children of "inferior" races and of the lower economic orders are incapable of high culture. We cannot fight elitism by unconsciously conforming the curriculum to that point of view. We must fight it by helping as many students as possible to become as sophisticated as possible, intellectually and emotionally. We must introduce the largest possible numbers to the argumentative advantages of clear, precise, forceful, imaginative, well-articulated speech and writing, and to all the arts of language that help us to become more fully and subtly aware of our feelings. The best is not too good for us common people. When we overcome our timidity, when we are not afraid to reach with our profane and merely human hands toward the treasures that have traditionally been called too good for us, when we stop accepting the conventional view that we are not good enough for them, we find that we too can too enjoy them. The capacity to enjoy them is not an external thing inherited by a few, like real estate or stock certificates; it is an innate capacity, like the capacity to learn to swim, and is more widespread than any elitist will ever admit; whether it is developed or remains forever latent depends on circumstance and opportunity, not on race or class, except where circumstance and opportunity are socially circumscribed by race or class.

This is precisely what elitists have always denied; and some egalitarians are so illiberal that between them and the elitists there is little to choose. Between the egalitarian Tolstoy, for example, who said in *What is Art?* that art that didn't help people to become morally better was bad, that he would give the peasants simple and morally edifying stories, poems, songs and pictures, but would condemn to the fire as "bad art" most of the treasures of European high culture, including for example the works of Bach, Handel, Mozart, Beethoven, Shakespeare, Swift, Balzac, Pushkin, and even (with the exception of two short stories) Tolstoy, because their intellectual, aesthetic and moral complexities were sources of corruption and required more education than the peasants had or than he wished them to have—education in complexities, subtleties and nuances being to his way of thinking corrupt education—

Where was I?

Ah yes. Tolstoy, the illiberal egalitarian. Between the egalitarian Tolstoy and the elitist Mallarmé, I was about to say, there is little to choose on this score. Mallarmé at age twenty was the very model of a snob, and he never advanced beyond the view he then expressed, though he never again expressed it so crudely. In the first and only essay of what was evidently intended to be a series, "Hérésies Artistiques: l'Art Pour Tous," he deplored the publication of good poetry in cheap edictions that made it available to large numbers of people, railed against "that impiety, the popularization of art," urged poets and musicians not to "open its arcana to the mob," said that literature should be kept out of the curriculum of public instruction since it was a divine "mystery" that could only be "profaned" by us common people, and concluded, "Let the masses read morality, but I beg you, don't give them our poetry to spoil."

In their conclusions, and in the practical effects that would have resulted if their ideas had prevailed, Mallarmé the avowed enemy of the people and Tolstoy the avowed friend of the people were remarkably similar. Surely the aim of democratic education must be neither to limit sophisticated instruction in the arts of language to a minority of students—a minority, as Mallarmé frankly put it, *de race,* of breeding, of good family—nor to level all students down to a common inarticulacy, but to educate everybody up to the maximum possible articulacy, freedom and joy in the use of language.

Nor can a democratic system of education, having such a purpose, accept the elitist assumption that the general capacity is low. Every morning, walking through a black slum on my way to Temple University, I pass the open door of a car-waxing garage whose walls are covered with pictures. Calendar pictures? No. Pin-up whores? No. Woolworth's embossed masterpieces? No. Impressionists. Monet.

Manet. Renoir. Degas. Morissot. Sisley. Van Gogh. Cézanne. Seurat. Pissarro. Vlaminck. Whistler. Turner. And recently in a railroad station I sat near a big middle-aged man in overalls, brogans and a locomotive engineer's cap, who was reading with physically evident enthusiasm a book. It was bound in limp black leather and printed in two-column format on thin paper with gold edges; in my wariness of religious fervor I assumed that he was working himself up into a fine access of zeal with Revelation or the Epistle to the Romans; but I thought that before moving out of range I should see just what it was that was affecting him in such a kinetic way, so I leaned closer and looked—and it was *The Tempest!*

*The Tempest!*

What would Mallarmé have thought of that? How could Tolstoy possibly have approved? But many who don't share either of their theoretical positions would side with them in this particular case and in any similar case—involving say "L'Allegro" or "Il Penseroso" or *Tristram Shandy* or *Cranford* or *The Private Papers of Henry Ryecroft* or *The Complete Works of A. O. Barnabooth.* Many would be tempted to ask of any of these, as of *The Tempest,* "Could anything be less relevant to the real needs of a locomotive engineer—or a college student? Could anything be less relevant to the needs of our time?" Our students do in fact ask such questions about many of the works we take up in class. The questions are themselves irrelevant, but they are asked so often, and with such innocent seriousness, that we must answer them. The answer of course is "Yes. Many current books on current issues are less relevant to the issues than *The Tempest* or *Cranford,* and less relevant to the real needs of locomotive engineers and college students and truck drivers and construction workers and file clerks and waitresses and small-business men and abused minorities and silent majorities. Jerry Rubin's *Do It!* is less relevant. (He would solve our problems by running around naked at political conventions and trying to out-clown the House Un-American Activities Committee. The Dadaists were doing that kind of thing back in 1919, and what good did it do?) LeRoi Jones's *Black Magic* is less relevant. (He would emancipate blacks by slaughtering white liberals, as if that were a workable program, and incidentally kicking Roy Wilkins in the ass. He offers to cure the deeply wounded blacks with the snake-oil of anti-Semitism, though he must know that the white trash who have been buying it for centuries remain uncured, unimproved and unassuaged. He hates Italians too, as if he were no better than Judge Webster Thayer or A. Lawrence Lowell. This is the insane poetry of a man whom racism has driven crazy with its own craziness.) In another direction, Stanley P. Wagner's *The End of Revolution* is less relevant. (He looks happily forward to the year 2000, when "the lust for travel" will replace the lust for acquisition and change the world accordingly.) Brian O'Leary's *The Making of an Astronaut* is less relevant. (Could anything be less relevant than that nice-boy way of life?) Shallowness is always irrelevant; that is the trouble with books in which the claims of propaganda override the claims of art and sense, or in which art and sense make no claims."

This is not to say that propaganda has no value. Certainly such novels as *Darkness at Noon* and *1984,* though they have no value as art, do dramatize and help to keep alive, for many readers who are not specially sensitive to the art of writing, the idea of personal freedom. Nor is it to say that the claims of art and propaganda never coincide. Certainly Robert Walser's *Jakob von Gunten* is excellent both as propaganda against servility and as a novel: it is a small but perfect masterpiece of literary art. Exactly the same thing can be said of Peter Weiss's *Exile.* And certainly Günter Grass's *The Tin Drum* and *Dog Years* are both persuasive propaganda and great novels. As Grass himself has said of *The Tin Drum,* "It's a political novel, but a novel, not politics."

Who would therefore condemn it? Only an enemy of personal freedom. We must not condemn works of art for not doing what they were not intended to do. To condemn a well-written play, poem or novel because it doesn't bear directly on our social-political-ecological problems is on a par with condemning an automobile because it isn't edible, or a potato because it doesn't provide transportation. To judge *The Tempest* by the standard of explicit concern with today's problems is to misjudge it and to lose its value. In many cases, such judgments involve the assumption that public problems are the only problems: an assumption as narrow as Tolstoy's that moral values are the only values.

We must recognize the limits of what art can do, and the high value of what it does within those limits. It can't feed us, it can't solve the problems of poverty and injustice, it can't bring peace or clean air or drinkable water; and there is no evidence that art or natural beauty makes anybody more humane—more perceptive morally or intellectually. Coleridge knew this. Plato knew it. We know now, moreover, that a hungry man has no intellectual interests and will not fight for freedom of the press against a dictator who promises to feed him, or reject on aesthetic grounds a tract or a cartoon that promotes the dictator's purposes. But we must not turn our backs on art because it is less important than food or because its action is no stronger than a flower. For we human beings, though we are animals first and last, are unique among animals in having a highly developed consciousness that enables us to see patterns and similarities and relations, to abstract and project and construct, not only by instinct but also by choice; and we are at the height of our humanity when we enjoy exercising these abilities. Art is the exercise of these abilities for the sake of our own joy in exercising them, with or without an ulterior purpose. Art is the joy of life. It is by nature free. It is the only absolute, pure and uniquely human freedom. Other things being equal, a person who has had some experience of it will be less easily coerced than one who hasn't. That's why conservatives have always hated free artists and opposed liberal education for the masses.

Joy is a value we undervalue at our political peril. Once we have experienced joy, we are much less satisfied with dullness; once we have joined in the joyful play of a lively mind, we are much less easily impressed by the stencils and stereotypes of a Presidential commercial. A waitress who has read and enjoyed *Cranford*—and she can read and enjoy it—is not so easily pushed around as one who hasn't. (That's why conservatives do everything to convince her that she can't.) A locomotive engineer who has read and enjoyed *The Tempest*—and I have seen one reading and enjoying it—is less liable than one who hasn't to be impressed by the Adam-Smithism of his employer or the racism of his union; a construction worker who has read and enjoyed *The Complete Works of A. O. Barnabooth*—and by what right would you say he can't?—is less liable than one who hasn't to yell "God bless the establishment!" or to be impressed by the wit of Spiro Agnew; a black student who has read and enjoyed *Tristram Shandy*—and I know several from stinking ghettos who have—is less liable than one who hasn't to be impressed by the crudities of LeRoi Jones.

The notion that joy and thought are enemies is as false as it is reactionary. That it is reactionary there can be no doubt, considering the novels (good as they are) of D. H. Lawrence, the poems (great as they are) of Yeats, the speeches (effective as they were) of Adolf Hitler, and the commercials (profitable as they may well be) of the R. J. Reynolds Tobacco Co. That the notion is false there can likewise be no doubt. We need only consider the tortured hatred that informs the major works of Lawrence and many of those of Yeats, and look around us at the desperately sad ecstatic faces of our students blowing their minds with loud, rocking, thumping, throbbing, thought-annihilating decibels—and of the anti-students blowing theirs, such as they are, with the ersatz orgasms of evangelistic fundamentalism. Escapists are never joyful, even in the midst of their escapes. And never free. Joy and freedom are born of clear and intense consciousness. Our most vital function as teachers is to promote a taste for art: for complexity, subtlety, nuance. Thus far we have failed, inasmuch as we have progressively watered down the curriculum as more and more people from homes without books have sought education, and inasmuch as we have been too timid or too politic or too disdainful to answer the demagogues who call the liberating arts "the bullshit subjicks." As long as we continue to fail, there will be an inarticulate majority for demagogues to appeal to.

# *Who Should Teach Freshman English?*

As a full professor, I am not supposed to teach freshman English; but I am allowed a section as indulgence of an eccentricity. "That's a rather expensive section," says a friend who is aware of administrative considerations. But that doesn't bother me, in fact I consider it quite right and proper, because I consider teaching freshman English the most important work I do.

My friend's gentle remonstrance is quite valid, given the situation as it is; but that only indicates the educational invalidity of the situation.

Why are most sections of freshman English taught by instructors and graduate assistants? The reasons are arithmetical and economic; they are not educational reasons. The large number of freshman sections makes it desirable from any administrator's point of view to teach them—or, as we say, to cover them—as cheaply as possible; and the relatively large numbers and easy availability of instructors and graduate assistants make it quite natural to use them for this purpose. "To use them." I quote. The cool impersonality of the phrase indicates the mechanical nature of this solution of the problem—a solution that largely ignores the living realities of the classroom hour and the office hour, the psychological problems of teaching freshmen.

The fact that a freshman section taught by a full professor is expensive is a fact no administrator can ignore; the fact that any considerable number of such sections is economically infeasible now, and in all probability will continue to be economically infeasible in any unideal future, is a fact we must all acknowledge; but the fact that the present arrangement is educationally undesirable is a fact to which we must not become reconciled.

Given the basic unalterability of the present arrangement, even by revolution—since by all accounts essentially the same arrangement prevails in Russia and in Communist China—what can we do to improve the intellectual and psychological conditions in our classrooms?

Whatever we do will cost a certain amount of money. Sophisticated administrators, who realize that they are running educational institutions, are willing to spend money in whatever amounts are feasible; Babbitty or Snopesian administrators, who think they are running businesses, are disappointed when any added expenditure for mere teaching turns out to be not infeasible. One long-range practical necessity, therefore, is for us teachers to organize to prevent the appointment of administrators whose values and purposes oppose our values and purposes, and to push aggressively for the appointment of men and women who understand what we are trying to do.

Simultaneously, and starting immediately, we in the two upper ranks must volunteer to teach freshman English, at least one section per year each, if not one section per term; we must push insistently for the maximum financially feasible number of us to be allowed to do so; and if the budgetary argument is used one-sidedly against us, we must ask insistently to see the budget (with proper names deleted). In most communities the local newspapers and newscasters are available to us as well as to administrators, and the threat or the fact of publicity can give some force to our insistence.

The fact that full and associate professors taught freshman English would raise both its status and its standards, and would give a lift to the morale of students and teachers alike. For the first time, we would be demonstrating in a practical way our recognition that freshman English is important; we would quickly re-learn, in case we had forgotten, that it is not the easiest but the hardest course to teach; and we would be reminded every day that the hardest course, which is also perhaps the most important single course, should not be left exclusively to the least experienced and the least knowledgeable teachers.

There is of course a reluctance in the two upper ranks to teach freshman English as it is now taught. But if any considerable number of us taught it, its nature would change. We would change it. Student evaluations of undergraduate courses are widespread now, and spreading wider; and in every case where I have asked I am told that the students consistently rate the older, more experienced teachers higher than the younger ones, and those with long lists of publications higher than those (regardless of age) who call themselves "devoted teachers." An undergraduate course taught by a scholar is thus demonstratably better, in the students' eyes, than a course with the same catalogue number taught by a beginner or by an old "devoted teacher" who neither writes nor reads. Thus freshman English taught by men and women who know enough to teach graduate courses would change, even if we made no conscious effort to change it; but of course we would make all kinds of conscious efforts, if only because we have lived too long to take that dreary useless trivial stuff seriously.

Effective teaching is done by example or not at all: and not so much by others' example as by our own. It is not true that he who can't teaches. He who can't merely goes through the motions of teaching. There are people who know all the rules in the rulebook and can diagram sentences like crazy, but who don't write well or even correctly; a "devoted teacher" whose prose is always dull, usually awkward and frequently ungrammatical can't teach anybody else to write with grace, precision, wit, clarity and force; the students themselves say that we who publish from time to time are better teachers than those who don't; and is it to be believed that a professional writer, such as Kay Boyle or William Gass or John Hawkes or Joyce Carol Oates or Peter de Vries, has less to give to students of creative writing, or less effective ways of presenting it, than some poor safe unimaginative slug who can only point out the rules in a stupid rulebook? Teaching doesn't keep these writers from writing; it doesn't keep us who are interested in our subject from writing publishable articles and books about it; and the most vital teaching we can do is to show freshmen the methods and devices of our own articulacy—not in order to have them write like us, but in order to lead them to develop their own methods and devices.

But what of the young instructors and graduate assistants whom we would displace? The solution is obvious. Let the young instructors fresh out of graduate school, who have just read the chief books and articles in their specialties, teach graduate courses; and let the graduate assistants teach literature to sophomores, juniors and seniors.

Let us discuss the less radical of these suggestions first. A graduate student preparing for oral or written exams at any level would certainly profit more by teaching a sophomore survey of English or American literature than by teaching freshman composition: he would profit both by the greater pertinence and sequentiality of the material and by the freedom from time-consuming correction of weekly themes; and a graduate student specializing say in the eighteenth century would certainly profit more by teaching an upper-division course, however general or special, in eighteenth-century literature. Since the two aspects of his work, learning and teaching, would be better integrated, he would teach more gladly and therefore probably better than he now does. At least, to whatever extent he was relieved of freshman classes, he would stop doing the harm he now does by his ignorance of the fundamentals of good writing. That particular vicious circle would be broken, at least in a few sections of freshman English. Doubtless a corresponding number of sophomores, juniors and seniors would be less well taught than they are now, but they would not be damaged as seriously as the freshmen are. The gain would surely be greater than the loss.

To the more radical proposal, that instructors fresh out of graduate school teach graduate courses, there are three principal objections.

The first is a professional matter. Certainly a new Ph.D. entering the job market, say as a Miltonist, and having to answer the question "With whom did you study Milton?" would have much better chances if he could respond with the name of a well-known

Miltonist, or at least of a scholar who had published several good articles on Milton, than if he had to respond with the unknown name of an instructor, however brilliant, whose brilliance was not yet visible beyond his own campus.

This is a completely valid objection. Therefore I can't with any validity deny it. To say that if the reform I propose were adopted the question "With whom did you study?" might in time cease to be asked is not very helpful or even consoling to those who must enter the job market while it is still being asked. Aside from the name-dropping, I'm afraid there can be no doubt that the real quality of graduate teaching in English would suffer for at least one college generation of four years. Such a sacrifice is not to be lightly consented to. But I believe with absolute faith that if freshman English did what it is supposed to do, the whole English program, including the graduate program, would be strengthened, and its quality raised.

The second principal objection has to do with the generation gap. A graduate assistant only five years older than his freshmen soon discovers that they are unaware of many things he takes for granted and that they consider him hopelessly old-fashioned and "out of it"; the difficulty, this argument runs, naturally increases with the age of the teacher; in graduate courses, on the other hand, since the students understand that the teacher's authority is not a convention but a reality, being the result of years of study, the generation gap is an asset; the lack of it might very well be a liability; and when—as would happen—some students were older than the teacher, the morale of the whole class would suffer.

This objection is less valid; in many cases, depending on the individual personality, it is not valid at all. In the first place, the generation gap in the classroom is a matter less of age than of expectations. Just as Americans traveling in Europe find the language barrier sometimes more baffling in England, where they expect to understand and be understood, than on the continent, where they don't, so freshmen are more surprised and dismayed by a gap of five years than by one of thirty. In the second place, freshmen do respond, if not to the reality of authority, certainly to its symbols, however invalid and merely conventional the symbols may be. Many a graduate assistant, vainly seeking to make the freshmen think of him or her as one of themselves, has disdained the symbols and so undermined his or her own authority. Back in the 1950's, when undergraduate girls wore bobby socks and saddle oxfords, I knew a beautiful and intelligent graduate assistant who also wore bobby socks and saddle oxfords. In her freshman classes she had very bad discipline problems. After trying every remedy, countermeasure and ploy she could think of, she confessed her despair to the department chairman. He smiled and said, "Get yourself some nylons and high heels and look like a grown woman and see what happens." She did, and the discipline problems ended immediately. So much for the generation gap.

The third principal objection has to do with public policy—and hence with internal administrative policy. A good university is not only a transmitter of old knowledge and received wisdom but also a producer of new knowledge and unheard-of ideas; without its productive function—without the research and speculation it permits—our knowledge would sink into mandarin obsolescence and our minds into medieval timidity: the kind of timidity that led Alcuin (735–804), at the beginning of every book he wrote, to assure his readers that it contained nothing new; the kind of timidity that led Hugh of Saint Victor (1096–1141) to recommend the cultivation of what he called "initial fear," the fear that operates in our inmost depths and makes it impossible for us to have an unorthodox thought.

All too many of us have this fear; the universities that encourage disinterested research and speculation keep it from being more widespread than it is; for thought can be kept alive only if knowledge increases. No living thing can be merely preserved or maintained: if it is not continually renewed and added to, if it doesn't grow, it declines and decays: if we were to declare, and could enforce, a moratorium on research for ten years—and some such silliness is in fact proposed from time to time—at the end of the ten years we would know considerably *less* than we do now: much of our information would have been forgotten, much of our skill would have been lost, from not having been used in pursuing new information and testing new ideas; and we would have sunk into the bad intellectual habit of accepting unexamined what learned authority tells us; we would have lost much of our capacity for independent observation—for seeing, free of prescribed preconceptions, what is before our eyes; and our thought would stiffen into superstition, in the sense in which John Stuart Mill used the word when he said, "Every new truth begins as heresy and ends as superstition."

The bad social effects of such a habit of mind cannot be overemphasized or exaggerated. So that research—the discovery of new facts, the correction of old theories in order to take account of new facts, and the elaboration of new ideas and new techniques that the new facts and new theories make possible—is vital to the health of society at large and to the health of teaching at all levels. So, quite aside from the financial cost, isn't it socially and educationally wasteful for productive scholars to teach elementary courses—in the case of English, for a teacher who is capable of solving puzzles presented by Shakespeare's or Joyce's texts, to spend his or her time correcting freshmen's grammar and spelling—work that could be done just as well by the unproductive? Or even by machines?

No. Freshman English is dull only when it is taught by dull people, or when bright young teachers are forced to teach it by the methods of dull old teachers. A productive scholar's mind is always active, and a change of direction from time to time, a new angle of vision, stimulates it to produce new ideas. Originality is largely a matter of association, of connecting things that were not previously connected; and this process is helped if we increase the number and variety of our associable experiences. Freshman English is full of what my wife calls unpredictable inspirations. Some of my happiest thoughts for sentences, phrases, rhythms, even whole articles, have come to me while I was straightening out the snarls and tangles of freshman prose or devising ways to make the Platonian elegance clear to the round unfocussed eyes of freshman innocence. The basic idea for an article on Samuel Beckett, which appeared in *The Hudson Review,* came to me while I was struggling to disenchant the deeply spellbound inarticulacy of a freshman engineering student by leading him through one of Beckett's periodic sentences; and some years earlier, by a circuitous but lightning-quick flash of associations, an ordinary grade C theme—in which a freshman girl was trying to shock me by telling me as vividly as her clichés would permit how much more she enjoyed sex with her current boyfriend than she had with her previous one—gave me the idea for an article that appeared in *PMLA* and later became the second chapter of my book on Joyce, *The Sympathetic Alien.*

Moreover, freshman English is hard enough to pique the ingenuity of the ablest teachers, and much too hard for most beginners to undertake successfully. The results of their unsuccess show up in our graduate courses—and even worse, in our public schools. Entering freshmen often introduce themselves with the apology, "Like English has always been my worst subject"; and junior, senior and graduate English majors have most difficulty not with understanding literature but with putting their thoughts and information on paper. Every teacher of graduate students of English is puzzled by the fact that many of them speak well or even brilliantly but write sloppily. When we read their doctoral dissertations we still have to correct errors of the kind we correct in freshman themes; and such errors often appear in the pages of the lesser learned journals.

Some years ago Roger Bacon said, "Too many men teach what they haven't learned." This is particularly true of teachers of freshman English. One of my duties as a teacher of remedial English two years ago was to go over themes the graduate assistants considered passable and see if they were indeed good enough to release their authors into English 1; and I was appalled by some of the "corrections" I saw. In one theme that I remember, the freshman had written a sentence about "children's games," and the graduate assistant had "corrected" it to read "childrens' games," conscientiously writing in the margin, " 'Children' is a plural form. In plural forms put the apostrophe after the s." In another, the freshman had written a bit of natural, believable dialogue in which a girl said to a boy, "I can't marry you, because I don't love you"; the graduate assistant had circled "can't" and "don't," and had written in the margin, "Do not use contractions." A person like that should have been strangled at birth.

But of course I'm not recommending strangulation as a general policy. My proposal that the best teachers should teach the hardest courses—the foundation courses—is not a radical but a reasonable and modest proposal, offered by way of reform, which along with reforms in our economic and social arrangements may save us from the mere destruction that revolution or counter-revolution or anarchy would bring. Freshman English as it is now taught doesn't work. It hasn't worked for a long time. In many cases it is simply being abandoned. This formal abdication of a responsibility we have long industriously neglected will not free us of it. The need for effective freshman English remains and grows; not to meet it is to acquiesce in the betrayal of the next generation—to deliver them tongue-tied and mind-weakened to the assaults of admen and political witch-doctors. The hard-won decencies of our culture—the right not to have our desks rifled by agents of the political party in office, the right not to have our mail opened by agents of the political party in office, the right to buy books by mail without having them thumbed through en route by agents of the political party in office, the right to talk on the telephone without being listened in on by agents of the political party in office, the right to disagree on matters of public policy without being accused of treason, the right not to have our personal worth denied because of our race or religion—will not survive our ability to think, speak and write clearly, or to judge the quality and significance of official statements. If the next generation continues its wordless descent into mere inarticulate feeling, it will soon be politically helpless. The enemies of reform are witting or unwitting advocates of Snopesian destruction.

# *Take for Example*
# Finnegans Wake

"The hiker I hilltapped the murk I mist my blezzard way." What kind of language is that? Language of the highest density, combining with the simple sentence "The higher I hilltopped the more I missed my blessed way" suggestions of hiking, tapping, murk, mist and blizzard, and also of "heeltap," which the *OED* defines as "1. A thickness or 'lift' of leather, etc. in a shoe-heel. 2. The liquor left at the bottom of a glass after drinking." Such is the language of *Finnegans Wake,* a novel that recounts in all their lightning-lit and thunder-blasted cloudy evasiveness the guilty dreams of a neurotic publican who, having drunk the heeltaps left by twelve customers, has fallen unconscious to the floor and been dragged upstairs to bed by his neurotic family.

Why read such a book? And why expose college students to it? Because it is a great book, both in its consummate artistry and in the scope of its vision. William York Tindall says *Ulysses* is the greatest novel ever written in English, with the possible exception of *Finnegans Wake;* when I read *Ulysses* I agree, but when I read *Finnegans Wake* I am inclined to reverse the order; certainly no other novel in English is within competitive distance of these two. In addition, *Finnegans Wake* has a technical virtuosity so astonishing that students always thrill to it—and anything we can do to make students thrill to good writing is all to the good. Of course Joyce didn't write *Finnegans Wake* as a textbook of composition, nor did Shakespeare write *Hamlet* as a textbook of composition; but we teachers have to take our examples of good writing where we find them, and more and more of us are coming to realize that in masterpieces we can find them unmixed with the dead prose in which most textbooks of composition are composed, and un-cluttered with the worse than useless rules with which they are cluttered.

"The scope of its vision," he said. What scope? What vision? What's so great about the dream-tormented night of a drunken publican? Well, his name is Humphrey Chimpden Earwicker, and his initials stand for Here Comes Everybody.

*Finnegans Wake* is a twentieth-century version of the oldest story in the world, Death and Resurrection. It is the story of Adam's fall and mankind's redemption, of Joseph's humiliation and triumph, of Jesus' descent into Hell and ascent into Heaven, of Dante's journey from night to morning, of the Autumn death and Spring reawakening of Persephone, of Bacchus, of Orpheus, of Adonis, of Osiris, of Mithra, of Baldur—of the many gods and heroes whose careers represent the revolution of the seasons, the alternation of day and night, the rise and fall of cultures and civilizations, the birth and death of individuals. In the seventeen years during which Joyce worked on his version, 1922 to 1939, we were "danzzling on the age of a vulcano," as he said: citizens of Danzig dancing bedazzled on the edge of a volcano in the age of Vulcan. We still are. The first copy of *Finnegans Wake* came off the press on Joyce's birthday, February 2, 1939; the official publication date—since it takes some time for reviewers to read a book and for bookstore managers to order it—was May 4; on May 7 Germany and Italy announced the military and political alliance that came to be known as the Berlin-Rome Axis; World War II, already obviously under way, began officially—with declarations, etc.—in September; Coventry was all but obliterated by bombing in 1940; the first atomic bombs were dropped in 1945. But Joyce had read Frederick Soddy's *The Chemistry of the Radioactive Elements,* and knew something of what was coming—including fallout and the poisoning of the air. In *Finnegans Wake* there is a discussion of weapons from the bow and arrow to "purefusion" (p. 222, lines 14—20—or, to give it the conventional notation we use, 222.14—20); a second passage (353.22—32), which includes the words "mulicules" and "moletons," says refugees from Coventry sit in London newsreel theaters, where "Similar scenatas are projectilised from Hullulullu, Bawlawayo, empyreal Raum and mordern Atems." (Here Imperial Rome is combined with the empyrean and the German word for space; "the modern Athens" is Edinburgh; "Mord" is the German word for murder, and "Atem," the German word for breath or breathing, also suggests, in this context, "atom.") A third passage (599.25—36) combines, for the benefit of "pacnincstricken humanity," the atomic cloud and the medieval Cloud of Unknowing: "between all the goings up and the whole of the comings down and the fog of the cloud in which we toil and the cloud of the fog under which we labour, bomb the thing's to be domb about it so that, beyond indicating the locality, it is felt that one cannot with advantage add a very great deal to the aforegoing." Such was Joyce's view of the snowed-out human picnic; and so much for the "relevance" of *Finnegans Wake,* if you must have relevance.

The picnic would go on for a long time nevertheless, Joyce believed: "Phall if you but will, rise you must: and none so soon either shall the pharce for the nunce come to a setdown secular phoenish" (4.15—17). (Whenever the word "finish" or any word suggesting "finish" occurs in *Finnegans Wake,* it also suggests "phoenix.") The human race would go on rising and falling, sometimes creating masterpieces of art, science, and social organization, sometimes being reduced to eating frogs' eggs for breakfast (12.14), "Till tree from tree, tree among trees, tree over tree become stone to stone, stone between stones, stone under stone for ever" (259.01—02).

The passages I have quoted, brief as they are, give us the clue to the book's greatness. This novel is 628 pages of pure poetry. Whatever significance its ideas may have—whatever "larger relevance" they may give the book—its relevance for us as English teachers lies in the brilliance of its language and structure and the breathing life of its characters. That is to say, its relevance for us is literary.

"There extand by now one thousand and one stories, all told, of the same" (5.28—29). Joyce begins with an Irish music-hall version: a comic song about a hod-carrier named Finnegan who has had a drop too much, falls from a scaffold, and thereby becomes the subject of a wake that evolves, under the influence of Ceres' distilled essence, into a rowdy party.—"And the all gianed in with the shoutmost shoviality" (6.18). "And of course all chimed din width the eatmost boviality" (58.14).—So that what with one thing and another a fight breaks out; one celebrant throws a bottle of whisky at another, who ducks; the bottle smashes against the wall; some of the divine elixir splashes on the recumbent form of Finnegan—and he rises up and roars, "Thunderin' Jazes! D'ye think I'm dead?"

As the individual's life epitomizes in little the life of the species, so the events of a single day epitomize the life of the individual. Joyce developed this theme in *Ulysses;* in *Finnegans Wake* he carries it forward into the night. The individual is not dead, but sleepeth; his life goes on in dreams, half-dreams, and unconscious reactions to stimuli from without and within. Here, in place of the Jew Leopold Bloom, we have another maladjusted Dubliner, the Protestant publican Humphrey Chimpden Earwicker, a Scandinavian with a hump on his back and a stutter in his mouth. He dreams about Finnegan; and shortly, as dreamers will, himself takes over the title role. As the dream progresses he identifies himself with Finn MacCool, the mythical giant on whose sleeping body Dublin rests; Cuchulain, who led an epic cattle raid in the early days of Ulster; Brian Boru, who drove the Danes from Ireland in 1014; Moses, Jesus, Allah, Shakespeare, Napoleon, Wellington, P. T. Barnum, and other heroes and great men, representing all human activities in all periods of history. He has had a day of humiliating failures in pursuit of unworthy objects, ending with his drunken fall to the floor. Moreover, he has been troubled lately by feelings of guilt arising from the diseased impulses of an unreflective man whose sexual potency is failing—"his craft ebbing" (290.27—28); all in all, he has a bad night. Following him through his unhappy six or eight hours, we ride the nightmare of contemporary history.

But he is more than one man, for he identifies with all the other members of his family: with his wife, Anna Livia Plurabelle; his daughter, Issy or Isobel or Isolde; his female servant, Kate the Slop, "built in with the bricks"; his twin sons, Shem and Shaun; and his departed manservant, whose name is not mentioned but who may be the Devil. Moreover, his wife, daughter and female servant tend to blend into each other, as well as into the great women of history and myth—Cleopatra, Theodora, Héloise, Marie Antoinette, Mme. de Pompadour, Mme. Blavatsky, Helen of Troy, Mary Magdalen, Joan of Arc, etc. His sons, however, fight all the time, because they represent opposing tendencies in his own nature: Shem the saint, Shaun the citizen; Shem the lover, Shaun the husband and father; Shem the poet, Shaun the publisher or publicist or critic or censor who in one way or another turns the poem to his own account; Shem the thinker, Shaun the professor who popularizes, misrepresents and appropriates his thought; Shem the offensive prophet, Shaun the politic priest; Shem the founder of a new religion, Shaun the priest of the old religion who kills Shem, but who when the new religion prevails turns out to be its chief priest and in its name kills Shem the heretic.

Their story goes round and round in "one continuous present tense" throughout all history (186.01) to make "the book of Doublends Jined" (20.15—16), which begins in the middle of a sentence and ends in the middle of a sentence. And since they are the whole human race, their language (though Joyce said it was "basically English") is intended to suggest the language of the whole human race as it might flow through the mind of a universal dreamer—a "Europasianised Afferyank" (191.04)—to whom all languages were as one. It includes words, idioms, phrases, clichés and proverbs not only from the familiar European and Asiatic languages but also from such little-known languages as Basque, Bêche-de-Mer, Bulgar, Esperanto, Kiswahili, Lithuanian, Malay, Romansch, Ruthenian, Shelta and Volapük. And there are other difficulties, including the profusion of literary, historical, theological, personal and *Kitsch* allusions, and the complexity of a structure in which every part has essential relations with every other part—a structure which, as Joyce says, he elaborated "with a meticulosity bordering on the insane" (173.34).

For this reason, and because the game seems well worth all our candles, there are thousands of pages of explication. In fact, the first book of explication. *Our Exagmination Round his Factification for Incamination of Work in Progress,* by Samuel Beckett and eleven other disciples, appeared in 1929—ten years before *Finnegans Wake* itself—and was reissued in 1961 (New Directions, $5). As one of its contributors, Victor Llona, said, "We commentators simply could not be kept in leash—we had to have our say in a volume which will grace the stalls in advance of the text under consideration." But it was not a matter of keeping them in leash. As fragments of his difficult new work began appearing in little magazines from 1924 onward, Joyce began preparing its potential readers by encouraging and even recruiting qualified critics to write about it. But since 1939 there has been no need for recruiting and no possibility of discouraging the joyful crowds of explicators, who include not only English teachers but also housewives, chemists, physicists, lawyers, opticians, musicians, painters, antique dealers, gentleman scholars and just plain nuts.

All their books and articles have in common a restricted subject and a wide range of reference. That is as it should be. Often the most fruitful fields for research are in those borderlands where two or more subjects become indistinguishable and we discover that it is impossible to draw sharp lines of demarcation between them. The more we know about a subject, the less ready we are to define it exactly; we gradually learn that in order to pursue our specialties we must make our education more general. The goal of a unified body of knowledge encompassing the natural sciences, the abstract sciences, the social sciences and the humanities seems almost impossibly distant, but within each of the major divisions there are unities: biochemistry, biophysics, physical chemistry; mathematical logic; social psychology; intellectual history, linguistic philosophy, aesthetics. Naturally, these borderlands are cultivated only by people who are at the frontiers of their own particular subjects. What I am saying is that there is no essential conflict between specialization and generalization: that in fact each is enriched by the other and necessary to the other.

A corollary is that even the most general reader of a major literary work is benefited by the special knowledge of specialists in fields other than literature, and that a literary scholar is even more insistently compelled to look outside his field. Since Dante, pleasant fellow, tended to put his enemies in Hell, his best friends in Heaven and everybody else in Purgatory, we can't read *The Divine Comedy* very intelligently without at least consulting the footnotes for details of late thirteenth- and early fourteenth-century Florentine politics; a little knowledge of theology and of mysticism doesn't hurt either; with how much more pleasure we can read of the intrigues at the court of Lilliput if we know something of those at the court of George I; and what don't we have to know to read *Finnegans Wake?* Specialists in contemporary literature find that they must venture into fields as seemingly unrelated as metaphysics and the structure of pineapples. The possibilities of superficiality and of self-deluding glibness are dismaying, but there is no help for it. We must venture or die. Consider: Alain Robbe-Griller, before he became a novelist, was an agronomist, a specialist in tropical fruits, and a propagandist who did much to popularize pineapples in France; in his novel *In the Labyrinth* a man lost in a strange city looks at a chipped and rusted street sign from which all but two letters are missing: "... NA ...". My guess is that the name of the street is L'ANANAS—PINEAPPLE—and that if we knew something about the structure of pineapples we would be able to see much more clearly than we now do the extremely complex relations of part to part in the novel, relations that involve its meaning. What folly! What mad pedantry! You see the risks we run.

But such risks are inherent in our enterprise; they cannot be avoided by anyone who is seriously concerned with contemporary literature; from day to day we put our very sanity on the line, and no one does so more cheerfully than do we Joyceans. For to investigate the strange and wonderful texts of the master is to step outside the safe boundaries of familiar literary study. The Joyce industry, as it is called, is indeed one of our most diversified intellectual enterprises; for Joyce was not only, as Eliot said, the greatest master of the English language since Milton, but also a supreme generalist, for a full understanding of whose works we would have to know not only at least nineteen languages, not only more European and Asiatic history than most of us know, not only more theological and ecclesiastical history than most of us know, not only more astronomy than most of us know, but also the history, folklore and mythology of Ireland in considerable detail, the history, topography and folklore of Dublin up to 1939 in seemingly exhaustive detail, the life cycle of the salmon, the alleged magical properties of cocoa, the doctrines and the methods of alchemy, the terminology of heraldry and falconry, the biographies of Joyce and many of his friends and relatives, and hundreds of odd facts dredged up from oblivion by the devoted industry of Joyceans whose specialty it is to seek the organizing principles that harmonize such disparities.

But don't be discouraged. I first came to it cold, not having read any of the scholarship, not knowing what it was all about, and was overwhelmed immediately with as much joy as puzzlement. Knowledge serves, but innocence also serves. We must become as little children, for they have no difficulty with *Finnegans Wake*. They have no taste: they can enjoy good writing as well as bad. Only with time and teaching do they learn to prefer the bad. Our first job as college teachers is to unteach them: to restore their innocence: and for this purpose *Finnegan Wake* is uniquely effective.

The discovery that it is not altogether inaccessible comes as a surprise even to graduate students who have read Joyce's other works; to freshmen who have not heard of Joyce it comes as the sudden recovery of a paralyzed sense, for it gives them for the first time since their pre-literate childhood the experience of a purely literary pleasure. Before a child learns to read, he can enjoy good language if he has a chance to hear it: "One misty moisty morning," "Cross patch, draw the latch," "Mistress Mary, quite contrary," and "Rig-a-jig-jig and away we go"; but in the first grade he learns with Dick and Jane and their dog Spot that language can be a joyless thing; and twelve years later, having had his taste developed by Lanier, Longfellow, Whittier, Freneau, John Masefield, Alfred Noyes, Rudyard Kipling, James Fenimore Cooper, Walter Scott, Conan Doyle, Booth Tarkington, Anthony Hope and Rafael Sabatini, together with bleached and degerminated versions of Dickens and Hardy by the likes of the authors of *Dick and Jane,* he goes to college and asks his English teacher, "Is Ayn Rand considered a good writer?"

There is no point in arguing with a person so horribly diseased. The only thing to do is to start curing him right away by exposing him to good language. Allopathy, I say. There are of course plenty of suitable specimens in contemporary literature—I may mention the description of Watt's clothes in Beckett's *Watt* (pp. 217–19), the account of the moon's passage in *Molloy* (pp. 51–52), some of Nabokov's stories, some of Nicolò Tucci's, some of Katherine Anne Porter's—but I have found that the Prankquean episode of *Finnegans Wake* (21.05–23.15) works best of all (see the appendix to this chapter).

It works so well because it presents an obvious challenge. One reading aloud suffices to show that it is not chaotic but has some kind of three-part pattern; after a second reading many students can see that the pattern is that of a fairy tale, and that in addition to the three main parts it has a coda, though they don't use that word; most of them begin to suspect that it has some meaning, if they could only somehow figure it out, and now and then one sees that the meaning inheres largely in the form, that to a large extent the form *is* the meaning. One said to me, "This is like a musical score: the conductor has to know where the theme is and who has it and what he must do with it." When a student reaches that point he is practically cured; for when he begins to think of what he reads in terms of form, he begins to have a sound base for literary judgment. I think, incidentally, that at least in the classroom we should avoid the word "taste," a metaphor of unaccountable subjectivity that makes literary judgment analogous to a preference for one kind of ice cream rather than another and misleads us into believing that there is really no way to tell good writing from bad. If I believed that—if I believed that my pleasure in Joyce was not demonstrably more valid than a freshman's in Ayn Rand—I would not presume to teach the art of reading or the art of writing. To be concerned with form is to be concerned with something demonstrable: a purely literary quality in terms of which one piece of writing is better than another. Concern with form is the beginning of judgment; and for making even the most naive students aware that there is such a thing, I have found the Prankquean episode uniquely valuable.

But *Finnegans Wake* as a whole is of course not for freshmen. It is for graduate students; and with them our purpose is not primarily to develop a consciousness of literary values but to gain some insight into the work at hand. *Finnegans Wake* immediately presents them with a simulating paradox: for they discover that it is not by any means virgin territory, that it was not virgin territory even when Harry Levin and Edmund Wilson first explored it, that in fact (Joyce's weapons being exile, cunning and publicity) it was never quite virgin territory, that nevertheless it remains largely unknown, and that—like nature itself—it will always by nature remain largely unknown.

For it is not fixed. It does not stand still for our inspection. Like every living book, it is fluid and endlessly evolving. Socrates' argument in *Phaedrus* that what is written down is fixed, dead and defenseless—an argument that the very setting of the dialogue mocks with its alter to Boreas, its reminders of Achelous, and its flowing Ilissus—all symbols of the Athenian loquacity and of Plato's own art, a flashing, shimmering iridescence that cannot with any fidelity be represented by a black-and-white diagram—

Where was I? Ah. Socrates' argument against writing down our living thoughts, an argument all around which *Phaedrus* flows, a living refutation, is refuted by every living book, and most especially by *Finnegans Wake,* which every generation must begin anew and every reader must approach anew each time he opens it.

Naturally we don't undertake to read the whole book in a school term. At the first meeting I lecture, by way of introducing the subject; at the second we read rapidly and superficially a number of passages in different styles, to get an idea of the book's stylistic variety, to see how themes are modulated to different purposes, and to glimpse the order in their gay profusion; then we settle down to book I, chapter 1, start reading it in as much detail as possible, and try to finish it by the end of the term. Sometimes we do finish it, sometimes we don't; in either case, we learn how to go about reading *Finnegans Wake.*

Between sessions we make use of all the guides and keys, all the list of names, songs, words, books, themes and motifs, the *Newslitter, The Analyst,*[1] the *OED,* Skeat's etymological dictionary,

---

1. *A Wake Newslitter,* edited by Fritz Senn and Clive Hart, Department

Grove's musical dictionary, and all the lexicons we are equipped to use; but when we bring our findings together we find that the act produces a qualitative innovation as radical as the occurrence of life in a carbon compound. For reading *Finnegans Wake* is a collective enterprise of no ordinary kind: what takes place is no mere quantitative gathering and mechanical assembling of parts into larger units, but a blending of objective and subjective elements—a kind of communion—in which one person's information calls up from another's subconscious an inference that validates the conjecture of a third. Joyce has revived the magical function of the old bards and shamans, in what by convention we consider a most unlikely place, the seminar room. If it should suddenly begin to rain in the room, I suppose we would all be surprised; still, it just might. Certainly we generate something in the nature of a ritual atmosphere. It is not surprising that Joyceans drink Guinness and John Jameson, go on pilgrimages, and publish memorial volumes; the impetus to such pieties comes from the sacred texts themselves.

The pedagogical problem is to stay within the limits of the demonstrable, beyond which lies if not madness at least silliness, without discouraging those happy intuitive leaps that in the best scholarship sometimes precede demonstration.

*Finnegans Wake* lends itself most happily; for its art is only an elaboration of principles that began to appear very early in Joyce's work. As William York Tindall has pointed out, the word "innumerous" in the last line of the poem "From dewy dreams, my soul, arise," means both "innumerable" and "not numerous"; but it also suggests the Latin *innumerosus,* unmelodious, inharmonious; Joyce uses the word "numerose" to describe Shaun's voice (*FW,* 407.17); and Tindall's observations on the disharmony of the last two lines of the poem support and are supported by my reading of the word.[2] In "The Sisters," the handkerchief with which the paralyzed priest tries to wipe away the stains of spilled snuff is "quite inefficacious." The word "ineffective" would have suggested the priest's physical debility just as clearly, but the theological word "inefficacious"

of English, University of Dundee, Scotland; *The Analyst,* Department of English, Northwestern University, Evanston, Illinois.
    2. *Chamber Music,* ed. William York Tindall (New York, 1954), pp. 199—200.

suggests spiritual debility as well, and also indicates the turn the narrator's mind has been given by the priest's instruction. Stephen Dedalus in the *Portrait* thinks of his raging sexual desire as "the luxury that was wasting him." "Luxury" here is an anglicization of *luxuria*, the official name of the deadly sin of lechery; by using this obsolete meaning of a modern English word, Joyce makes more poignant Stephen's conviction of sin and also indicates very early the pedantic tendency of the boy's mind: there is a hint of self-mockery even here. These examples suggest that the early works are "difficult" in essentially the same way that *Finnegans Wake* is difficult. The difference is one of degree: in the earlier works the difficulty is not great once we see it, but it is unobtrusive and insidious, so that we may miss a point without suspecting that we have missed anything; in *Finnegans Wake* the difficulty is both more obvious and more difficult, being compounded through a multiplicity of languages and elaborated with boisterous virtuosity.

Paul Valéry's twentieth-century Faust describes its magical quality quite clearly:

> I want to produce a great work, a book. . . . It would be an intimate blending of my true and false memories, of my ideas, of my previsions, of hypotheses, of valid inferences, of visionary experiments: all my diverse voices! A reader could enter it at any point and leave it at any point. . . . Perhaps no one will read it, but anyone who does will never be able to read another book. . . . I want to write it in a style of my own invention, which will permit me to pass miraculously back and forth from the bizarre to the common, from absolute fantasy to extreme rigor, from prose to verse, from the flattest platitude to the most . . . the most fragile ideas. . . . A style, in short, that will unite all the modulations of the soul and all the leaps of the mind; and which, like the mind itself, will sometimes run back over what it is expressing in order to feel itself being expressed and recognize itself as the will to expression, the living body of that which speaks, the awakening of thought, which is suddenly astonished that it could ever have been confused about anything, though such confusion is precisely its essence and its role.[3]

That is unmistakably the style of *Finnegans Wake*. Mephistopheles calls it "Mephistophelean." But it is not one style but

---

3. Paul Valéry, *Mon Faust*, (Paris, 1946), pp. 48–50. My translation.

many; for its nature, as defined by its purpose, is multiplicity itself. We should expect it to be less a style than a medley of styles, and in merely talented hands to be perhaps unavoidably cheap. The charge of acrobatic cheapness was in fact one of the commonplaces of commonplace criticism in the early years of *Ulysses;* even serious critics have said that *Ulysses* ran chiefly to parody and pastiche; conversely, it was for a long time assumed that *Finnegans Wake* was written in one style; and even now we hardly know what to make of its variety.

What I make of it provisionally is an interpretation so un-orthodox that I present it to my students—and now to the readers of this volume—with some hesitancy. Harry Levin's insight that the publican HCE could not be the dreamer because he lacks the education to have such a dream[4] gives us our clue: the narrator is always somebody who could be the narrator of the particular passage in question. I believe that just as in *Ulysses* each character thinks, talks and is described in his own style, so in *Finnegans Wake* every change of style indicates that another person, awake or half-awake or asleep as they sit up with the body, is dreaming or being dreamed about. They are all HCE. However, since they dream about each other, it is often difficult to tell who is the current dreamer or narrator and who is a character in his dream or narration.

This is the way we provisionally interpret book I, chapter 1, in my classes. It seems to explain some things that need explaining. In the first place, though the book begins and ends in the middle of a sentence, the second half of the sentence (3) has a style so different from that of the first half (628) that it seems not to be spoken by the same person. The first half brings an intensely lyrical passage to a climax with the iambic rhythm of copulation: "A way a lone a last a loved a long the"—at this point the coition is interrupted—one of Joyce's obsessive jokes—and the second half of the sentence has the

---

4. Harry Levin, *James Joyce: A Critical Introduction,* (Norfolk, 1941 and 1960), p. 175. Clive Hart, in *Structure and Motif in Finnegans Wake,* pp. 78–82, discusses various conjectures as to the dreamer's identity. I see no necessary conflict between the single-dreamer and multiple-dreamer theories. In *A Portrait of the Artist as a Young Man* the woman who invited Davin in for the night and the girl who tried to sell Stephen flowers were one and two and more than two.

tone of a lecture: "riverrun, past Eve and Adam's, from swerve of shore to bend of bay, brings us by a commodius vicus of recirculation back to Howth Castle and Environs." Perhaps what we have here after all is not one sentence but fragments of two different sentences, so that *Finnegans Wake,* like the world, ends in the dark nothingness from which it emerged, and what we have is not a circle but a relatively small visible segment of a large invisible circle or ellipse or spiral or repetitive scrawl. This view enhances the grandeur of Joyce's conception. However that may be, the incomplete sentence with which the book ends is certainly spoken by Anna Livia, and the incomplete sentence with which it begins is certainly not. At the end Anna is losing her identity in that of her father-husband-sons, and the professorial tone of the opening fragment comes from him: not from the river but from the sea, not from our great sweet mother but from our great bitter father. "Mearmerge two races [flows of water], swete and brack" (17.24). The all-inclusive sea, our comprehensive Old Father Ocean (627–28), speaks with the voice of Shaun or Shem or Anna or Isobel or the Four Masters or the Twelve Apostles or Adam or Eve or Jonathan Swift or Brillat-Savarin or the Duke of Wellington: like the Neo-Platonic God of Dionysius the Areopagite or Nicholas of Cusa, HCE is Everybody and Everything.[5]

The first narrator, who talks as if he stood with a lectern before him, a map behind him, and a pointer in his hand, is most probably Shaun; learning is not inconsistent with Shaun's character, and the vulgar tone of the whole lecture seems to be his. On p. 8 he breaks off the lecture and takes us to the museum, where the janitrix or genetrix, Kate the Slop, Goddess of Battles, shows us through. However, since after we leave the museum Shaun still has us in charge, it is likely that he continues to be the dreamer all through the museum passage (8.09–10.23), mocking Kate as his literary ancestor Buck Mulligan mocks Mother Grogan. Likewise in the Mutt and Jute episode (15.29–18.16), it is not the voices of Mutt and

---

5. In his lecture on Shakespeare in *Ulysses,* Stephen Dedalus makes the same point: "We walk through ourselves, meeting robbers, ghosts, giants, old men, young men, wives, widows, brothers-in-love. But always meeting ourselves" (213 [210]).

Jute that we hear but the voice of Professor Shaun, composing an imaginary interview (something professors have been known to do) and putting into his characters' supposedly primitive mouths allusions to the Stone Age, strong and weak verbs, Viconian cycles, a Wagnerian song, Tacitus' history and Wood's coinage scheme. After Mutt and Jute the lecture proper is resumed, and with the exception of a brief passage in which Shem speaks (19.31–20.18), is continued until Finnegan wakes (24.15). At this point it is suddenly broken off, the style changes abruptly, and what follows is not a lecture but a series of impromptu speeches by people at the wake, urging Finnegan to lie down and accept death, telling him that he would not care for the world as it is now, assuring him that procreation, building and destruction are being carried on as usual by his descendants, and comforting each other with the brave notion that not they but he "will be ultimendly respunchable"—that he is Adam and God but they fortunately are not.

To determine who each of these deluded souls is would require a long, detailed stylistic analysis—which I for one, having other things to do, shall not undertake at any time that I can foresee. But I hope that others will agree and be moved to do it. Doubtless it would be a collective undertaking. In the reading of *Finnegans Wake,* everybody teaches everybody else.

## *Appendix: THE PRANKQUEAN—* *A FAIRY TALE*

The numbers in the margin indicate pages and lines in the text of *Finnegans Wake:* 21.05 means page 21, line 5. The numbers under the lines are intended to help us locate verbal motifs: the first motif occurs at 21.05, 21.33 and 22.21.

It was of a night, late, lang time agone, in an auldstane eld,  21.05
    1 1 1 1 1 1 1 1 1 1 1 1 1

when Adam was delvin and his madameen spinning watersilts,

when mulk mountynotty man was everybully and the first leal

ribberrobber that ever had her ainway everybuddy to his love-

saking eyes and everybilly lived alove with everybiddy else, and
2  2

21.10    Jarl van Hoother had his burnt head high up in his lamphouse,
2  2  2  2  2  2  2  2  2  2  2  2  2  2  2  2  2  2  2  2  2  2  2  2  2

laying cold hands on himself. And his two little jiminies, cousins
2  2  2  2  2  2  2  2  2  2  2  3  3  3  3  3  3  3  3  3  3  3  3  3  3

of ourn, Tristopher and Hilary, were kickaheeling their dummy
3  3  3  3  3  3  3  3  3  3  3  3  3  3  3  3  3  3  3  3  3  3  3  3  3

on the oil cloth flure of his homerigh, castle and earthenhouse.
3  3  3  3  3  3  3  3  3  3  3  3  3  3  3  3  3  3  3  3  3  3  3  3  3

And, be dermot, who come to the keep of his inn only the neice-
4  4  4  4  4  4  4  4  4  4  4  4  4  4  4  4  4  4  4  4  4  4  4  4  4

21.15    of-his-in-law, the prankquean. And the prankquean pulled a rosy
4  4  4  4  4  4  4  4  4  4  4  4  4  5  5  5  5  5  5  5  5  5  5  5  5  5

one and made her wit foreninst the dour. And she lit up and fire-
5  5  5  5  5  5  5  5  5  5  5  5  5  5  5  5  5  5  5  5  5  5  5  5  5

land was ablaze. And spoke she to the dour in her petty perusi-
5  5  5  5  5  5  5  6  6  6  6  6  6  6  6  6  6  6  6  6  6  6  6  6  6

enne: Mark the Wans, why do I am alook alike a poss of porter-
6  6  6  6  6  6  6  6  6  6  6  6  6  6  6  6  6  6  6  6  6  6  6  6  6

pease? And that was how the skirtmisshes began. But the dour
6  6  6  7  7  7  7  7  7  7  7  7  7  7  7  7  7  7  7  8  8  8  8  8  8

21.20    handworded her grace in dootch nossow: Shut! So her grace
8  8  8  8  8  8  8  8  8  8  8  8  8  8  8  8  8  8  8  9  9  9  9  9

o'malice kidsnapped up the jiminy Tristopher and into the shan-
9  9  9  9  9  9  9  9  9  9  9  9  9  9  9  9  9  9  9  9  9  9  9  9  9

dy westerness she rain, rain, rain. And Jarl van Hoother war-
9  9  9  9  9  9  9  9  9  9  9  9  9  10  10  10  10  10  10  10  10

lessed after her with soft dovesgall: Stop deef stop come back to
10  10  10  10  10  10  10  10  10  10  10  10  10  10  10  10  10  10  10

my earin stop. But she swaradid to him: Unlikelihud. And there
10  10  10  10  10  10  10  10  10  10  10  10  10  10  10  11  11  11

21.25    was a brannewail that same sabboath night of falling angles some-
11  11  11  11  11  11  11  11  11  11  11  11  11  11  11  11  11  11

where in Erio. And the prankquean went for her forty years'
11 11 11 11 12 12 12 12 12 12 12 12 12 12 12 12 12

walk in Tourlemonde and she washed the blessings of the love-
12 12 12 12 12 12 12 12 12 12 12 12 12 12 12 12 12

spots off the jiminy with soap sulliver suddles and she had her
12 12 12 12 12 12 12 12 12 12 12 12 12 12 12 12 12

four owlers masters for to tauch him his tickles and she convor-
12 12 12 12 12 12 12 12 12 12 12 12 12 12 12 12 12

ted him to the onesure allgood and he became a luderman. So then                    21.30
12 12 12 12 12 12 12 12 12 12 12 12 12 12 12 12 12  4 4 4 4

she started to rain and to rain and, be redtom, she was back again
4 4 4 4 4 4 4 4 4 4 4 4 4 4 4 4 4 4 4 4 4 4 4 4 4 4 4 4

at Jarl van Hoother's in a brace of samers and the jiminy with
4 4 4 4 4 4 4 4 4 4 4 4 4 4 4 4 4 4 4 4 4 4 4 4 4 4 4 4

her in her pinafrond, lace at night, at another time. And where
4 4 4 4 4 4 4 4 4 1 1 1 1 1 1 1 1 1 1 1 1 1 4 4 4 4 4

did she come but to the bar of his bristolry. And Jarl von Hoo-
4 4 4 4 4 4 4 4 4 4 4 4 4 4 4 4 4 4 4 2 2 2 2 2 2 2 2

ther had his baretholobruised heels drowned in his cellarmalt,                    21.35
2 2 2 2 2 2 2 2 2 2 2 2 2 2 2 2 2 2 2 2 2 2 2 2 2 2 2 2

shaking warm hands with himself and the jiminy Hilary and
2 2 2 2 2 2 2 2 2 2 2 2 2 2 23 3 3 3 3 3 3 3 3 3 3

the dummy in their first infancy were below on the tearsheet,                    22.01
3 3 3 3 3 3 3 3 3 3 3 3 3 3 3 3 3 3 3 3 3 3 3 3 3 3

wringing and coughing, like brodhar and histher. And the prank-
3 3 3 3 3 3 3 3 3 3 3 3 3 3 3 3 3 3 3 3 3 5 5 5 5 5 5 5

quean nipped a paly one and lit up again and redcocks flew flack-
5 5 5 5 5 5 5 5 5 5 5 5 5 5 5 5 5 5 5 5 5 5 5 5 5 5 5

ering from the hillcombs. And she made her witter before the
5 5 5 5 5 5 5 5 5 5 5 5 5 5 5 5 5 5 5 5 5 5 5 5 5 5 5

wicked, saying: Mark the Twy, why do I am alook alike two poss                    22.05
5 5 5 5 6 6 6 6 6 6 6 6 6 6 6 6 6 6 6 6 6 6 6 6 6 6 6

of porterpease? And: Shut! says the wicked, handwording her
6 6 6 6 6 6 6 8 8 8 8 8 8 8 8 8 8 8 8 8 8 8 8 8 8 8 8

madesty. So her madesty a forethought set down a jiminy and
8 8 8 8 9 9 9 9 9 9 9 9 9 9 9 9 9 9 9 9 9 9 9 9 9 9 9 9 9 9

took up a jiminy and all the lilipath ways to Woeman's land she
9 9 9 9 9 9 9 9 9 9 9 9 9 9 9 9 9 9 9 9 9 9 9 9 9 9 9 9 9 9

rain, rain, rain. And Jarl von Hoother bleethered atter her with
9 9 9 9 9 9 9 10 10 10 10 10 10 10 10 10 10 10 10 10 10

22.10 a loud finegale: Stop domb stop come back with my earring stop.
10 10 10 10 10 10 10 10 10 10 10 10 10 10 10 10 10 10 10 10

But the prankquean swaradid: Am liking it. And there was a wild
10 10 10 10 10 10 10 10 10 10 10 10 11 11 11 11 11 11

old grannewwail that laurency night of starshootings somewhere
11 11 11 11 11 11 11 11 11 11 11 11 11 11 11 11 11 11

in Erio. And the prankquean went for her forty years' walk in
11 11  12 12 12 12 12 12 12 12 12 12 12 12 12 12 12 12

Turnlemeem and she punched the curses of cromcruwell with
12 12 12 12 12 12 12 12 12 12 12 12 12 12 12 12 12

22.15 the nail of a top into the jiminy and she had her four larksical
12 12 12 12 12 12 12 12 12 12 12 12 12 12 12 12 12

monitrix to touch him his tears and she provorted him to the
12 12 12 12 12 12 12 12 12 12 12 12 12 12 12 12 12

onecertain allsecure and he became a tristian. So then she started
12 12 12 12 12 12 12 12 12 12 12 12 12 12 4 4 4 4 4 4 4 4
ı
raining, raining, and in a pair of changers, be dom ter, she was
4 4 4 4 4 4 4 4 4 4 4 4 4 4 4 4 4 4 4 4 4 4 4 4 4 4 4 4

back again at Jarl von Hoother's and the Larryhill with her under
4 4 4 4 4 4 4 4 4 4 4 4 4 4 4 4 4 4 4 4 4 4 4 4 4 4 4 4

22.20 her abromette. And why would she halt at all if not by the ward
4 4 4 4 4 4 4 4 4 4 4 4 4 4 4 4 4 4 4 4 4 4 4 4 4 4 4 4

of his mansionhome of another nice lace for the third charm?
4 4 4 4 4 4 4 4 4 1 1 1 1 1 1 1 1 1 1 1 1 1 1 1 1 1 1

And Jarl von Hoother had his hurricane hips up to his pantry-
2 2 2 2 2 2 2 2 2 2 2 2 2 2 2 2 2 2 2 2 2 2 2 2 2 2 2

box, ruminating in his holdfour stomachs (Dare! O dare!), and
2 2 2 2 2 2 2 2 2 2 2 2 2 2 2 2 2 2 2 2 2 2 2 2 3 3

the jiminy Toughertrees and the dummy were belove on the
3 3 3 3 3 3 3 3 3 3 3 3 3 3 3 3 3 3 3 3 3 3 3 3 3

watercloth, kissing and spitting, and roguing and poghuing, like          22.25
3 3 3 3 3 3 3 3 3 3 3 3 3 3 3 3 3 3 3 3 3 3 3 3 3

knavepaltry and naivebride and in their second infancy. And the
3 3 3 3 3 3 3 3 3 3 3 3 3 3 3 3 3 3 3 3 3 3 3 3 5 5 5 5

prankquean picked a blank and lit out and the valleys lay twink-
5 5 5 5 5 5 5 5 5 5 5 5 5 5 5 5 5 5 5 5 5 5 5 5 5 5

ling. And she made her wittest in front of the arkway of trihump,
5 5 5 5 5 5 5 5 5 5 5 5 5 5 5 5 5 5 5 5 5 5 5 5 5 5

asking: Mark the Tris, why do I am alook alike three poss of por-
6 6 6 6 6 6 6 6 6 6 6 6 6 6 6 6 6 6 6 6 6 6 6 6 6 6

ter pease? But that was how the skirtmishes endupped. For like          22.30
6 6 6 6 6 7 7 7 7 7 7 7 7 7 7 7 7 7 7 7 7 7 7 7 7

the campbells acoming with a fork lance of lightning, Jarl von

Hoother Boanerges himself, the old terror of the dames, came

hip hop handihap out through the pikeopened arkway of his

three shuttoned castles, in his broadginger hat and his civic chol-

lar and his allabuff hemmed and his bullbraggin soxangloves          22.35

and his ladbrook breeks and his cattegut bandolair and his fur-

framed panuncular cumbottes like a rudd yellan gruebleen or-          23.01

angeman in his violet indigonation, to the whole longth of the

strong of his bowman's bill. And he clopped his rude hand to

his eacy hitch and he ordurd and his thick spch spck for her to
                            8 8 8 8 8 8 8 8 8 8 8 8 8 8 8

shut up shop, dappy. And the duppy shot the shutter clup (Per-          23.05
8 8 8 8 8 8 8 8 8 8 8 8 8 8 8 8 8 8 8 8 8 8 8 8 8 8

kodhuskurunbarggruauyagokgorlayorgromgrammitghundhurth-

rumathunaradidillifaititillibumullunukkunun!) And they all drank

free. For one man in his armour was a fat match always for any

girls under shurts. And that was the first peace of illiterative
7 7 7 7 7

23.10  porthery in all the flamend floody flatuous world. How kirssy the
7 7 7 7 7 7 7

tiler made a sweet unclose to the Narwhealian captol. Saw fore
7 7 7 7 7 7 7 7 7 7 7 7 7 7 7 7 7 7 7 7 7 7 7 7 7 7 7

shalt thou sea. Betoun ye and be. The prankquean was to hold
7 7 7 7 7

her dummyship and the jiminies was to keep the peacewave

and van Hoother was to git the wind up. Thus the hearsomeness

of the burger felicitates the whole of the polis.

The Prankquean's riddle occurs from time to time throughout *Finnegans Wake:* unmistakably at 21.18, 22.05, 22.29, 223.23, 224.14, 260.05, 301F1, 311.22, 317.22, 324.12, 365.34, 372.04, 417.07, 493.29 and 623.14, and possibly at 38.05, 466.30 and 511.19. (Don't worry about that "301F1." In the conventional notation of *Finnegans Wake* studies, it means "page 301, footnote 1.")